Washington County
Tennessee

Superior Court Minutes

1791-1804

Compiled By:

Work Progresss Administration

Please direct all correspondence and orders to:

www.southernhistoricalpress.com
or
SOUTHERN HISTORICAL PRESS, Inc.
PO BOX 1267
375 West Broad Street
Greenville, SC   29601
southernhistoricalpress@gmail.com

ISBN #0-89308-879-X

Printed in the United States of America

(p-1)   FEBRUARY TERM 1791

At a Court of Equity began and held for the District of Washington
within the Territory of the United States of America South of the River
Ohio in the Courthouse of the County of Washington on Tuesday the fifteenth
day of February one thousand seven hundred & ninety one.
    Present
            The Honble
                    David Campbell)
                          &   ) Esqrs
                    John McNairy   )

Andrew Russell produced a commissions which is the words following to wit:
William Blont Governor in and over the Territory of United States of America
South of the River Ohio. To all who shall see these presents greeting:
Know ye that I do appoint Andrew Russell of the County of Washington in the
said Territory Clerk and Master in Equity of the Superior for the District
of Washington and do authorize and impower him to execute and fulfil the
duties of that Office according to Law and to have and to hold the said
office during his good behaviour or during the existence of the Temporary
Government of the said Territory with all the priviledges and Emoluments
to the same of Right appertaining. Given under my hand and seal in the
said Territory this twenty seventh day of October in the year of our Lord
one thousand seven hundred & ninety. Signed Wm. Blont . By the Governor
Rich Mitchel with a certificate thereon that he had taken an oath to support
the Constitution of the United States and ----- Oath of office.
(p-2)
Tuesday the 22nd day of February 1791.
    Present The Honble
                    David Campbell)
                          &   ) Esquires Judges
                    John McNairy   )
Alexander Hamilton ------------------plt.)
          Against   ) In Equity
James Patterson --------------------deft.)

    By Consent of the parties by their attornies . It is ordered that
Commissions issue to take the depositions of the witnesses in this cause on
giving the adverse party thirty days previous notice of the time and place
of executing the commissions to examine those witnesses which reside out of
the District, and ten days previous notice to those who reside within the
District.

    John Williams of Granville County Esquire; ----------------------------
----------James Hogg of Orange County Gentleman Thomas Hart of ------- County
in the State of Maryland Merchant----------------and David Hart of Caswell
County, Gentlemen --------------plts.

against) In Equity
The heirs and Devisees of Richard Henderson late of Granville County Esquire deceased; of Nathaniel Hart of ------ County in Virginia Gentleman
decd of William Johnston late ------ Orange County merchant decd; of John
Lutteral   (p-3)   and Leonard H. Bullock late of Chatham County Gentleman deceased de----

    John Umstead, Susanna Umstead, Leonard H. Bullock, Richard Henderson
one of the heirs and devisees of Richard Henderson decd. A. Henderson ,
Spruce Macoy, Fanny Macoy, John Henderson, by Archibald Henderson his
Guardian and Elizabeth Henderson by Spruce Macoy her Guardian having acknowledged the service of the Copy of the bill and Subpeona in this Cause
and they failing to appear and put in their answers or pleas agreeable
to the Rules in Chancery or demur; The said bill as to them is taken for
confessed and appointed to be heard exparte at the next Court.

    And the rest of the said heirs and Devisees not having entered their
appearance according to the rules of this Court, and it appearing to the
satisfaction of the Court that they reside without the limits of this
Territory. On the motion of the plts. by their attorney it is ordered
that unless the said heirs & Devisees shall appear here on the first day
of the next term and answer the bill of the plts. that then it shall be
taken for confessed, and that a copy of this order be forthwith published
in the Cape Fare Gazette with sixty days from this time, and in the newspaper regularly published in the District of Kentucky for three weeks
successively and at the door of the Court house in the Town of Jonesboro.

(p-4)   George Martin ------------- plt.)
           against   ) In Equity
    Andrew English -------------deft.)

    By consent of the parties by their attornies.. It is ordered that
commissions issue to examine and take the depositions of the witnesses in
this cause giving the opposite party ten days previous notice of the time
and place of executing the same.

William Nelson --------------------- plt.)
    against   ) In Equity
John Hannah ---------------------deft.)

    By consent of the parties by their attornies. It is ordered that
commissions issue to examine and take the depositions of the witnesses in
this cause giving the opposite party twenty days previous notice of the time
and place of executing the same.

Henry Massingal --------------plt.)
    against   ) In Equity
David Hughes & James Stuart ---defts.)

    By consent of the parties by their attornies. It is ordered that com-
missions issue to examine and take the depositions of the witnesses in
this cause giving the opposite party ten days previous notice of the time
and place of executing the same.
    Thursday 24th February 1791.
        Present the same Judges as before.

(p-5)   Samuel Baughman ------- plt.   )
                       against   )   In Equity
           Vachel Dellingham & John Woods - defts.)

     By consent of the parties by their attornies. It is ordered that commissions issue to examine and take the depositions of the witnesses in this cause, giving the opposite party twenty days previous notice of the time and place of executing the same; and that John Dunkam and George Vincent be commissioners for this purpose in Sullivan County; Henry Woods & George Sammons in the County of Greenville in South Carolina, and that Thomas Payne and Benjamin Ekles in the county of Washington in Georgia. And it is further ordered that Vachel Dellingham the deft. give Security in the Sum of one hundred pounds to abide by & perform the Decree of this Court.

William Blevins & others   -   plts.)
           against   ) In Equity
John Shelby   -   deft.)

William Blevins & others   -   plts.)
           against   ) In Equity
John Shelby   -   deft.)

William Blevins   -   plt.)
           against   ) In Equity
John Brown   -   deft.)

John Shelby   -   plt.)
           against   ) In Equity
William Blevins & others   -   defts.)

(p-6)   Den on the Demise of John Shelby plt.)
                 against   ) In Equity
         William Blevins & others defts.   ) By consent

     On the Motion of John Shelby and John Brown defts by their attorney in the foregoing suits in Equity it is ordered that other sufficient security be given for the prosecution of the said suits in the sum of four hundred pounds. And on the Motion of the said Blevins & others by their attorney It is ordered that the said Shelby and Brown be bound in the sum of four hundred pounds current money to abide by and perform the Decree of the Court in the said suits. And by agreement of the parties by their attornies the Jury of view in the Cause in Ejectment is discharged from their attendance until the eighth day of the next term; that those depositions which have heretofore been taken by the parties on ten days notice shall never be excepted to by either party on account of not having longer notice and that commissions shall issue to take the depositions of the rest of the witnesses in these causes on giving the adverse party legal notice of the time and place of executing the same. And for reasons appearing to the Court. It is ordered that these causes be continued till the next term.

(p-7)   Simon Kukendol   --- plt.)
            against   )   In Equity
       Robert McAffee   ----deft.)

For reasons appearing to the Court. It is ordered that this Cause be continued till the next term.

David McPeters and Charles McDowell - plts.   )
           against   ) In Equity
Alexander Outlaw, Martin Caswell and John Herritage - defts.)

By consent of the parties by their atta. It is ordered that this
cause be continued till the next term; and that commissions issue to examine
and take the depositions of the witnesses in this cause giving the adverse
party legal notice of the time and place of executing the same.

John Adair   -   plt.)
  against   ) Equity
Edmund Williams -   deft.)

By consent of the parties by their attornies. It is ordered that this
cause be continued till the next term.

John Aaronwine - plt.)
   against   ) Equity
John Shelby   - deft.)

By consent of the parties by their attornies. (p-8) It is ordered
that John Hackett a Surveyor for the plt. and Joseph Greer for the deft.
attend and run out and Survey the lands in dispute agreeable to the bounds
and lines expressed in each party's title and make three accurate plans of
such Surveys and return the same to the next Court.

Charles Hays   -   plt.)
   against   )Equity
Samuel Harris   -   deft.)

For reasons appearing to the Court, It is ordered that this cause be
continued till the next term, and that a commission issue on behalf of the
deft. to Burk County to examine and take the deposition of witnesses in
this cause on giving the plt. legal notice of the time and place of executing
the same.

George Martin   -   plt.)
   against   ) Equity
Andrew English -   deft.)

William Nelson   -   plt.)
   against   ) Equity
John Hannah   -   deft.)

For reasons appearing to the Court. It is ordered that these suits
be contd. till the next Court, and by consent of the parties. It is agreed
that no exceptions shall be taken to depositions heretofore taken on (p-9)
ten days previous notice.

John Tadlock   -   plt.)
   against   ) Equity
Isaac Rutland   -   deft.)

By consent of the parties by their attornies. It is ordered that this
cause be continued till the next term, and that commissions issue to examine
and take the depositions of the witnesses in this cause, giving the opposite

party legal notice of the time and place of executing the same.

Alexander Hamilton   -   plt.)
      against   ) Equity
James Patterson   - deft.)

    By consent of the parties. It is ordered that this cause be continued till the next term, and that other and better security be given by the plt. for the presecution of this cause.

Henry Massingal   -   plt.   )
      against   ) Equity
David Hughes & James Stuart - defts.)

    By consent of the parties by their attornies. It is ordered that this Cause be continued till the next term and that Francis A. Ramsey a Surveyor for the deft. and Joseph Greer a Surveyor for the plt. attend and run out and Survey the lands in dispute agreeable to the lines and bounds expressed in each party's title, and make three accurate plans of such Surveys and return   (p-10)   the same to the next Court.

Ruth Brown   -   plt.)
    against   ) Injunction in
John McDowell   - deft.) Equity

    For reasons appearing to the Court it is ordered that this Bill of Injunction be dismissed.

John Bull   -   plt.)
    against   ) Equity
Benjamin Goodwin   -   deft.)

    James Stinson deputy Sheriff of Greene County having made affidavit that he served the deft. with a copy of the bill and taken his body on a writ of capias in proper time and he failing to appear and put in his answer or plea agreeable to the rules in Chancery, or demur; the said Bill is therefore taken for confessed and appointed to be heard exparte at the next term.

John Waddel   -   plt.)
    against   ) Equity
Robt. Patterson   -   deft.)

    Time is given the deft till the next term to put in his answer.
              David Campbell, J. T. U. S.
              John McNairy, J. T. U. S. S. R. O.
AUGUST TERM 1791

(p-11)   At a Court of Equity Begun and held at the court house in Jonesborough the 15th day of August 1791 for the District of Washington in the Territory of the United States South of the River Ohio.

              Present the Honble
                    David Campbell)   Esqrs.
                          &   )   Judges
                    Joseph Anderson)

```
John Tadlock      -   Complt. )
      agst.                    ) On an Injunction in Chancery
Isaac Bullard     -   deft.   )
```

By consent of the parties. It is ordered that this suit be dismissed
at the cost of the complt the deft having previously acknowledged satisfaction for the Debt mentioned in the complts Bill.

Andrew Russell Clerk and Master in Equity entered into and acknowledged
his Bond according to Lots which Bond is in the words following to wit:
Know all men by these presents that Andrew Russell, Alexander Outlaw, John
Rhea and Joseph Love -----------are held and firmly bound unto the honorable David Campbell, John McNairy, and Joseph Anderson Esquires, Judges in
and over the Territory of the United States South of the River Ohio and
to their Successors in office in the sum of Two Thousand pounds current
money: To the payment where of to be made to the said Judges and their
successors in office we bind ourselves, our heirs, executors and administrators jointly and severally firmly by these presents, Sealed with our
seals and dated this 23rd day of August 1791.

The Condition of the above Obligation is such that whereas the above
bound Andrew Russell hath been constituted and appointed Clerk and Master
in Equity for the District of Washington in the sd Territory by commissions
from his Excellency William Blount Esqr. bearing date the 27th day of
October 1790. If therefore the said Andrew Russell shall   (p-12)
safely keep the Records of the Court of Equity for the said District of
Washington and shall faithfully discharge his duty in Office then the
above Obligation to be void otherwise to remain in full force and Virtue.
Andrew Russell (L.S.) Alexr Outlaw (L.S.) John Rhea (L.S.) Josiah
Love (L.S.)

```
Richard Brindle   - Complainant )
      agst.                     ) Injunction
Caleb Carter      - Defendant   )
```

The attorney for the complainant having produced an order signed by
the deft and attested by two witnesses directing this suit to be dismissed
at his costs. For these reasons It is ordered by the Court accordingly.

```
Simon Kerkydale   - complainant )
    against                     ) Injunction
Robert McAffee    -  Deft       )
```

For reasons appearing to the Court. It is ordered that this cause
be continued till the next term.

```
David McPeters and Charles McDowell  - Compt.              )
            agst.                                          ) Chancery
Alexander Outlaw, Martin Caswell and John Herritage - defts.)
```

For reasons appearing to the court. It is ordered that this cause
be continued till the next term.

```
John Waddel       -   complt. )
      agst.                   ) Equity
Robert Patterson  -   deft.   )
```

Time is given the deft till next November Court to put in his answer.

```
John Adair         ---     complt. )
       against                      )    Injunction
Edmund Williams    --      deft.   )
```

For reasons appearing to the Court. It is ordered that this cause be continued till the next term and it is ordered that commissions be awarded the parties to examine and take the depositions of the witnesses in this cause giving legal notice of the time and place of executing the same.

```
(p-13)   John Aaronwine -- complainant )
                 against               )    Equity
         John Shelby    -- defendant   )
```

For reasons appearing to the Court. It is ordered that this cause be continued till the next term.; and that commissions be awarded the parties to examine and take the depositions of the witnesses in this cause on giving legal notice of the time and place of executing the same.

```
Charles Hays       --      complainant )
  against                              )
Samuel Harris      --      defendant   )
```

For reasons appearing to the Court. It is ordered that this cause be continued till the next term; and that commissions be awarded to the parties to examine and take the depositions of the witnesses in this cause on giving legal notice of the time and place of executing the same, complts notice to the defts attorney to be sufficient.

```
Samuel Baughman    ---   complt.           )
   against                                 )    Equity
Vachel Dellingham & John Wood  --- defts. )
```

By consent of the parties by their attornies. It is ordered that this cause be dismissed at the costs of the complainants.

```
William Blevens    ---   complainant )
       against                       )    Equity
John Brown         ---   deft.       )
```

By consent of the parties by their attornies. It is ordered that the probat of the defts answer be sufficient.

```
Alexander Hamilton --- Complainant )
       against                     )    Equity
James Patterson    ---- deft.      )
```

The Deft. having departed this life will the commencement of this suit It is ordered that the same be abated and that a seirefacias issue against the executors or administrators of the said decedent to revive the said suit.

```
(p-14)   William Nelson --  complainant )
                 against                )    Equity
         John Hannah    ---- defendant  )
```

For reasons appearing to the Court It is ordered that this Cause be continued till the next term.

Henry Massingal   —   complainant)
        against   )   Equity
David Stuart and James Stuart - defts.)

By consent of the parties by their attornies. It is ordered that this cause be continued till the next term, and that commissions are awarded the parties to examine and take the depositions of the witnesses in this cause giving legal notice of the time and place of executing the same. And it is ordered that Joseph Greer a Surveyor for the complainant and Francis Alexander Ramsey a Surveyor for the deft run out and Survey the Lands in dispute agreeable to the lines and bounds expressed in each party's Title and make three accurate plans of such Surveys and return the same to the next Court.

David McPeters and Charles McDowell - complt.   )
            agst.   )   Equity
Alexander Outlaw, John Herritage and Martin Caswell - Defts.)

For reasons appearing to the Court. It is ordered that Jas. Galbreath Surveyor for plts. & F. A. Ramsey for defts run out and Survey the lands in dispute included in the Grant obtained by John Herritage for six hundred and forty acres in Greene County on the North side of Nolachucky joining Martin Caswell including the mouth of flat creek and one other by Martin Caswell for the same quantity on the North side of Nolachucky joining an Entry made in the name of Pharioh Cobb.

William Cox   —   complt.)
        agst.   )   Equity
Augustine Brumley -   Deft.)

By consent of the parties. It is ordered that this cause   (p-15) be continued till the next court and that commissions be awarded the parties to examine and take the depositions of the witnesses giving legal notice of the time and place of executing the same.

John Williams Esquire of Granville County, James Hogg of Orange County Gentleman Thomas Hart of ------ County in the State of Maryland Merchant and David Hart of Caswell County Gentlemen ------- Complt.
                    against) Equity
The heirs and Devisees of Richard Henderson late of Granville County Esqr deceased of Nathaniel Hart of ----- County in Virginia Gentleman decd of William Johnston late of Orange County Merchant decd of John Lutteral of Chatham County Gentleman decd & Leonard H. Bullock ------- defts.

Some of the said Heirs and Devisees having failed to enter their appearance according to the Rules of this Court and it appearing to the satisfaction of the Court that they reside without the limits of this Territory. On the motion of the ------ by their attorney it is ordered that unless the said heirs and Devisees shall appear here on the first day of the next term and answer the bill of the complainants that then it shall be taken for confessed and that a copy of this order be forthwith inserted in the Cape Fare Gazette the Kentucky Gazette and Knoxville Gazette and the Newspapers regularly Published in Hagerstown for three weeks successively and at the door of the court house in the Town of Jonesboro.

George Martin   -   complt.)
   against   )   Equity
Andrew English   -   def't.)

For reasons appearing to the Court. It is ordered that other sufficient security be given for the prosecution of this suit.

William Blevins and others - complt.)
       agst.   )   Equity
John Shelby   -- deft.)

This day came the parties by their attornies and   (p-16)   thereupon came also a Jury to wit. Joseph Britton, Landon Carter, Joseph Conway, Henry Conway, William Conway, John Sevier, William Trimble, John Blair, Jesse Hoskins, William Horner, Asabel Rollings, & Wyat Stubblefield, who being sworn well and truly to enquire "whether the lands in dispute between the parties were ever known to be in the County of Augusta in the State of Virginia" upon their oath do say that the land in dispute never Lay in the State of Virginia in the County of Augusta.

And the aforesaid Jurors being sworn well and truly to enquire "whether the Government of Virginia did exercise or assume Jurisdiction on the North side of Holstein including the lands in dispute between the parties at the time of the Grant in the year 1753 & from that time until the extending the line in 1779, or at any time during that period" upon their oath do say that the government of Virginia did assume ----- exercise Jurisdiction on the North side of Holston including the lands in dispute between the parties.

And the aforesaid Jurors being sworn well and truly to enquire "whether the lands claimed by the complainants are those covered by the old patent Grant under which the deft. claims" upon their Oath do say that the lands claimed by the complts. are those covered by the old patent grant under which the defts. claim, and it is ordered that this cause be continued till the next term and that commissions be awarded the parties to examine & take the depositions of the witnesses in this cause giving legal notice of the time.

Samuel Wilson   -   plt.   )   Upon a motion for failing
    agst.   )   to execute a process on
Thomas Berry Sheriff of Hawkins - deft.)   E. Walden.

For reasons appearing to the Court it is ordered that the deft. be fined fifty pounds current money Ni Si Ordered that notices to the attornies at Law who reside without the limits of this Territory shall be good & legal(rest of page pasted over)

(p-17) Simon Kirkeyndale - complainant)
       against   )   Equity
    Robert McAffee   -   deft.)

For reasons appearing to the Court. It is ordered that unless the said deft. shall appear here on the first day of the next term that then the sd. Complts. bill shall be taken for confessed and It is ordered that a copy of this order be forthwith inserted in the Knoxville Gazette (if any be published) for three weeks successively and at the door of the Court house in Jonesboro.

William Nelson   -   complt.)
   against   )   Equity
John Hannah   -   deft.)

On the motion of the parties by their <u>attornies</u> It is ordered that
commissions be awarded them to examine and take the depositions of the
witnesses in this cause, giving legal notice of the time and place of
executing the same.

Samuel Willson   -   complt.)
    against   )   Equity
Elisha Walden   -   deft.)

The deft. having filed his plea in abatement of the complainants bill
on arguments whereof It is ordered that the complainants bill be dismissed
at the costs of the complainant, and it is ordered that this suit be contd.
as an original Bill in Equity.

George Martin   -   complt.)
   agst.   )   Equity,
Andrew English   -   deft.)

For reasons appearing to the Court It is ordered that this cause be
continued till the next term, and that commissions be awarded the plt. to
examine and take the depositions of the witnesses in this cause giving
legal notice of the time and place of executing the same, and the same for
the deft. according to the written application of his attorney & that
notice to the complts attorney shall be sufficient.

(p-18)   John Bull   -   complt.)
         agst.   )   Equity
     Benjamin Goodwin -   deft.)

This cause was heard exparte upon the bill of the complt; which is
in the words following "North Carolina Washington District Superior Court
of Equity August term A. D. 1790. To the honorable the Judges of the
Superior Court of Equity" on consideration whereof It is ordered and Decreed
that the several bills of Sale for the property of John Bull complt. given
to the deft. Benjamin Goodwin be annulled & made void for fraud practised
by the said deft in obtaining the same, that the said deft be decreed to
bring the said Bills of Sale into this Court to be annulled that the deft
restore to the said Complt the several articles of his property mentioned in
the same Bill of Sale and that the said deft. pay to the said complt. the
sum of four pounds thirteen shillings & four pence in restitution for the
sum of three pounds ten shillings Virginia money fraudulently obtained by
the said deft. of and from the complt. on a false void & fraudulent pretence
of having an Entry for the improved Lands of the sd. complt. in the Gap
of Bays Mountain & that the complt. recover his costs.

And it is ordered that an attachment be awarded agst. the deft. to
enforce the foregoing Decree and it is further ordered that a Sciafacias
issue agst. his <u>securitys</u>.

David McPeters & Charles McDowell - Complts.   )
            against   )   Equity
Alexander Outlaw, John Herritage & Martin Caswell - defts.)

On the motion of the defts. by their attorney It is ordered that
other sufficient security be given for the prosecution of this suit.

And for reasons appearing to the Court It is ordered that unless the
defts. John Herritage & the heirs of Martin Caswell shall appear here on
the first day of the next term that then the bill of the complts. be taken
for   (p-19)   confessed, and that acopy of this order be forthwith published in the Cape Fear Gazette & the Knoxville Gazette for four weeks
successively and at the door of the court house in the Town of Jonesboro.

Ordered that the Court be adjourned till Court in Counsel

(p-21)   FEBRUARY TERM 1792

At a Court of Equity Begun and held in the Town of Jonesborough the
fifteenth day of February one thousand seven hundred & ninety two for the
District of Washington in the Territory of the United States of America
South of the River Ohio
            Present
                The Honorable,
                    David Campbell   )
                    Joseph Anderson)   Esquires
                        &   )   Judges
                    John McNairy   )

James Bryant   -   complt.   )   Upon a writ of
    agst.   )   Injunction & a
James Houston, Alexander Outlaw   )   Bill in Equity
& the heirs of Joseph Bullard decd. - defts.)

On the motion of the defendants by their council and for reasons
appearing to the Court It is ordered that the writs of Injunction obtained
by the complainant against James Houston and the heirs of Joseph Bullard
decd to stay the proceedings at Law mentioned in his Bill of Complaint
be dissolved and that the sd. defts. James Houston & their heirs of Joseph
Bullard decd recover their costs.

And on the motion of the complainant by his council, It is ordered
that the Bill of Complaint exhibited in this cause be continued as an
Original Bill.

Samuel Wilson   -   plt.)   Upon a Bill contd.
    against   )   as an Original Bill by an Order
Elisha Walden   -   deft.)   of Court after the dissolution of the
                                 Writ of Injunction.
By directions of the Plts. attorney It is ordered that this suit be
dismissed.

(p-22) John Bull   -   plt.   ) Upon a Writ of
            agst.   ) Scerefacias upon a
        Caleb Carter and Alexander Goodman - Defts.) Bond entered into by
                                    the said Defts. with Benjamin Goodwin the
                                    25th day of October 1790 for the appearance
                                    of the said Benjamin Goodwin at the suit

of the plt. in Equity, on the 15th day
of February 1791 at the Court house in
the Town of Jonesborough.

fifa issued to shff.
of Green

This day came the plt. by his attorney and the said defts. being solemnly
failed to appear; Therefore It is considered by the Court that the plt. have
execution against the said defts. for the sum of four pounds thirteen shillings
and four pence the sum in the Decree obtained by the plt. against the aforesaid Benjamin Goodwin at the last Term, and the costs by him expended in the
prosecution of his suit aforesaid here.

William Blevins & others - complts.)
                agst.   ) Two Suits in Equity
John Shelby   - Deft.   )

    For reasons appearing to the Court; It is ordered that these suits be
continued till the next term, and that Publication of the Testimony be passed
on the first day of May next. -- And on the motion of the deft. by his
attorney It is ordered that a commission be awarded him to examine and take
the deposition of Mr. John Fawler in Kentucky on giving the complts. thirty
days previous notice of the time and place of executing the same.-- And
on the motion of the complts. by their attorney It is ordered that commissions
be awarded them to examine and take the depositions of their witnesses in
these suits on giving the deft. Legal notice of the time and place of
executing the same.

(p-23)   William Blevins --- complt.)
                agst.   ) Equity
          John Brown   --- Deft.)

    For reasons appearing to the Court It is ordered that this suit be
continued till the next term and that commissions be awarded the parties to
examine and take the depositions of their witnesses in this cause, giving
the advarse party legal notice of the time and place of executing the same,
and that publication of Testimony be passed on the first day of May next.

Peter McCall   ---- Complt.)
         against   ) In Equity
John Fagan   ---- Deft.)

    By consent of the parties by their attornies, all matters in difference
between them are referred to the determination of Gilbert Christian, John
Long, George Maxwell and Abraham McClallon and in case of disagreement they
are to choose & umpire whose award is to be made the Decree of this Court
and the same is ordered accordingly.

David McPeters & Charles McDowell - complts.   )
                agst.   )
John Herritage, Martin Caswell and Alexander Outlaw - Defts.)

    The Demurrer of the deft Martin Caswell to the Bill of the complainant
being heard upon the arguments of the counsel on both sides It seems to the
Court, here that the sd complts. Bill and the subject matter therein continued

are insufficient in Law for them the said complts. to maintain their said
Bill of complaint against the said deft. neither is he compelled to put
in any further or other answer to the same.

Therefore It is considered by the Court that the complts take nothing
by their said Bill of complaint, but that the said deft be hence dismissed
with his costs by him about his defence in this behalf expended.

And the Demurrer of John Herritage to   (p=24)   the Bill of the
complts being heard upon the arguments of the counsel on both sides being
heard. It seems to the court here that the said complts bill and the facts
therein contained are sufficient in Law for them the said complts to maintain their said Bill of complaint against the said deft. John Herritage and
that he is compelled to put in a further answer there to,--- And on the
prayer of the said deft. John Herritage by his counsel time is given him till
the next term to put in his answer.

And on the motion of the parties commissions are awarded them to
examine and take the depositions of their witnesses on giving the adverse
party legal notice of the time & place of executing the same.

An Instrument of writing was exhibited in Court which is in the words
following "whereas Evan Shelby hath Bought the improvements and tract of Land
of John Cox where he now lives and if the Patents granted to John Buchanan
where Collo Preston & William Campbell now executors for the said Buchanan's
estate and if the said patent for the said should be broke or vicated and
the said land to be vacant and no other elder rights so that the said Shelby
should have liberty to take rights for the said land either in Virginia or
North Carolina and gett patents there for, then said Shelby is to pay to
John Cox Fifty pounds Virginia cur'y as well as thirty pounds already paid
in hand. In witness whereof I have hereinto gett my hand and seal this 4th
day of February 1773. Evan Shelb y (L.S.) Signed sealed in the presence of
John Fowler and John Shelby". And was proven by the Oath of John Shelby
a subscribing witness thereto and ordered to be recorded.

(p-25)   John Adair   -   complt.)
              agst.   )   In Equity
          Edmund Williams -   deft.)

For reasons appearing to the Court, It is ordered that this cause be
continued till the next term, and that Publication of the Testimony pass.

John Aaronwine   -   complt.)
    agst.   )   In equity
John Shelby   -   deft.)

For reasons appearing to the Court, It is ordered that this cause be
continued till the next term, and that commissions be awarded the parties to
examine and take the depositions of their witnesses, giving Legal notice to
the adverse party of the time and place of executing the same, which commissions shall be executed within five months at the expiration of which time
it is ordered that publication of the Testimony do pass.

Charles Hays   -   complt.)
              agst.   )   In Equity
Samuel Harris   -   Deft.   )

For reasons appearing to the Court It is ordered that this suit be continued till the next term, and that commissions be awarded the parties to examine and take the depositions of the witnesses in this cause giving Legal notice of the time & place to the adverse party of the time and place of executing the same, which commissions shall be executed within five months, at the expiration of which time it is ordered that publication of the Testimony do pass.

```
Alexander Hamilton  -    complt.)
             agst.             )        Equity
Robert Patterson    -    deft.  )
```

Ordered that Scerifacias issue to revive the proceedings in this cause.

(p-26)   John Williams Esqr. of Granville County,
James Hogg, of Orange County,
Gent. Thomas Hart of   County,
in the State of Maryland, merchant and David Hart of Caswell County
Gent.   -   Complts.
             agst.   ) In Equity
The heirs and devisees of Richard Henderson, late of Granville County
decd of Nathaniel Hart of   County in Virginia Gent: decd of
William Johnston, late of Orange County Merchant decd. of John Lutteral
of Chatham County Gentleman, decd and Leonard Hl Bullock -   Defts.

Some of the said heirs and devisees having failed to enter their appearance according to the Rules of this Court, and it appearing to the Satisfaction of the Court, that they reside without the limits of this Territory: on the motion of the said complts. by their attornies. It is ordered that unless the said heirs and devisees shall appear here on the first day of the next term and answer the Bill of the complts. that then it shall be taken for confessed, and it is ordered that a copy of this Order be forthwith inserted in the Kentucky Gazette and the newspaper regular published in Hagerstown for three weeks successively and at the frot door of the Court house in the town of Jonesborough.

```
John Shelby      -----  Complt.)
             agst. -----      )Instituted by consent
William Blevins ------- Deft.  )
```

For reasons appearing to the Court It is ordered that this cause be continued till the next term.

```
Den on the Demise of John Shelby    -  plt.  )
             agst.                            )  Eject.
William Blevins & others            -  defts. )
```

For reasons appearing to the Court It is ordered that this cause be continued till the next term.

```
(p-27)   George Martin      ----    complt.)
             agst.                         )  Equity
         Andrew English     -----   Deft.  )
```

For reasons appearing to the Court, It is ordered that this suit be continued till the next term, and that commissions be awarded the parties

to examine and take the depositions of the witnesses in this cause giving
legal notice to the advarse party of the time and place of executing the
same, which commissions Shall be executed within five months, at the expiration of which time publication of the Testimony shall pass.

William Nelson   -   complt.)
              agst.   )   Equity
John Hannah   -   Deft.)

For reasons appearing to the Court, It is ordered that this suit be
continued till the next term, and that commissions be awarded the parties to
examine and take the depositions of the witnesses, giving legal notice of
the time and place of the executing the same.

Henry Massingal   -   complt.)
              agst.   )   Equity
David Hughes & James Stuart - Deft.)

For reasons appearing to the court It is ordered that this cause be
continued till the next term, and that commissions be awarded to examine
& take the depositions of the witnesses in this cause giving the advarse
party Legal notice of the time and place of executing the same.

And it is ordered that Francis A. Ramsey a Surveyor for the deft. and
Jos. Greer a Surveyor for the complt. run out and Survey the lands in Dispute agreeably to the lines & bounds expressed in each party's title, and
make out three accurate plans of such Survey and return the same to the
next term.
(p-28)
John Waddel   -   complt.)
              agst.   )   Equity
James Patterson -   Deft.)

On the motion of the deft by his atta. time is giving him till tomorrow morning to put in his answer.

William Cox   -   complt.)
              agst.   )   Equity
Augustine Brumley -   deft.)

For reasons appearing to the Court It is ordered that this cause be
continued till the next term, and that commissions be awarded the parties
to examine and take the depositions of the witnesses in this cause giving
the advarse party legal notice of the time & place of executing the same.

Moses Humphreys   -   complt.)
              agst.   )   Equity
Matthew Talbott   -   Deft.)

For reasons appearing to the Court It is ordered that this cause be
continued till the next term, and that commissions be awarded to examine and
take the deposition of the witnesses in this suit, giving the advarse party
legal notice of the time and place of executing the same.

George Mitchel   -   complt.)
              Agst.   )   Bill & Injunction
John Carney   -   deft.)

The deft having filed his answer td the bill of the complt. on the
motion of the said deft. by his attorney. It is ordered that the injunction
obtained by the complt. agst. the deft. to stay the proceedings at Law upon
a Judgment obtained by the said deft. agst. the complt. at the last Superior
Court for the District of Washington in the   (p-29)   Territory of the
United States of America South of the River Ohio for eighty Pounds Current
money and costs be disabled, and the said complt. pay the costs in this
behalf expended.

William Ashert son and heir at Law
to William Ashert dedd.   ----   complt.   )
              agst.   )   Equity
John Cox Senr. John Cox Junr. and Thomas Amis - deft.)

Samuel Wilson   -   complt.)
              agst.   )   Equity
Elisha Walden   -   Deft.)

Robert Kerr   -   complt.)
              agst.   )   Equity
Alexander Meek   -   Deft.)

John Vance   -   complt.)
              agst.   ) Equity
John Laughlin & Robert Craig Exers of the last will & Testament)
of John Laughlin decd. - Defts.)

     For reasons appearing to the Court it is ordered that the defts. in
the foregoing suits have time till the next term to put in their answers.

Samuel Smith   -   complt.)
              agst.   )   Equity
Philip Saunders admr.-   defts.)

     For reasons appearing to the Court It is ordered that the Bill of the
Complt. be taken for confessed and that it be appointed to be heard exparte
at the next term.

(p-30)   James Bryant   -   complt.)
              agst.   )
         James Houston the heirs of   )   Equity
         Joseph Bullard decd, and   )
         Alexander Outlaw -   Defts.)

     The Demurrers of the said defts. to the Bill of the Complt. being
heard upon the Arguments of the Council on both sides. It seems to the
Court here that the matters of fact alledged by the complt. as they are
set forth by himself are insufficient for him to proceed upon or to oblige
the said defts to make answer unto.

     Therefore it is considered by the Court that the said defts shall not
be compelled to make any other answer to the said Bill of complt. and that
the said defts. recover their costs by them in this behalf expended.

David Booths   -   complt.)
              agst.   )
Benjamin Ford & Gerrett Fitzgernald - defts.)

The Demurrer of the Defts. to the Bill of the complt. being heard upon
the Arguments of the counsel on both sides, and because the court will advise
thereupon. It is continued till the next Term.

John Waddell   -   complt.)
            agst.   ) Equity
Robert Patterson   -   Deft.)

    The deft. having filed his answer on the motion of the parties by their
attornies it is ordered that commissions be awarded them to examine and take
the depositions of their witnesses in this suit.
(p-31)
An Instrument of writing from Peter Turney to Robt. Sevier was exhibited in
Court which is in the words following know all men by these presents that
I Peter Turney of Fincastle County have bargained and sold unto Robert Sevier
of the said place one certain place and improvement of Land lying between
the Lands of Roger Tapp, John Shelby & John Beler the said price of Land I
the said Turney purchased from John Beler now I the said Peter Turney do
assign over & now deliver up all my right Title claim and demand of the said
Land and improvement unto the said Robert Sevier as it being for value
Received of him Witness my hand & seal this ninth day of February 1774 Peter
Turney (L.S.) Witness present John Sevier, Robert Stuart. With an as-
signment thereon which is in the following words "I assign over unto Mr.
John Shelby all my right Title claim and demand of the within Bill of Sale
as witness my hand this ninth day of February 1774 Robert Sevier (L.S.)
witness present John Sevier and Robert Stuart" and proven by the oath the
said John Sevier a subscribing witness thereto and ordered to be recorded.

Simon Kerkendall   -   Complt.)
            agst.   ) Bill & Injunction
Robert McAffee   -   deft.)

    Publication having been made in the Knoxville Gazette pursuant to the
order of the court made at the last term, and it appearing from the Testimony
of Joseph Hadin & Charles Robinson Esqrs. that the full amount of the
Judgment to which the Injunction in this cause was obtained was paid to the
said deft. on consideration whereof it is Decreed and ordered that the
Injunction aforesaid be made perpetual and that the complt. be ajoined from
recovering the Judgment at Law mentioned in this Bill of Complt. and that
the complt. pay the costs in this behalf expended   (p-32)   and have
execution agst. the sd. deft. for the same.

David McPeters & Charles McDowell   -   complt   )
            agst.   ) Equity
John Eerritage, Martin Caswell & Alexander Outlaw - Defts.)

    On the motion of the defts. by their Counsel it is ordered that a
commission be awarded to take the affidavit of John Eerritage to his answer
to the Bill of the complts. directed to the Honble John Litgreaves.

    And it is further ordered that the Bill be referred to the Clerk &
Master, and that he report whether the name of the deft. Martin Caswell
be erased together with the necessary alterations consequent on such
erasure, or remain as it now stands in the sd. Bill.

```
Samuel Wilson      -    plt. )   Upon a Rule
        agst.                )       to shew cause
Thomas Berry       -    deft. )   why he should
```
not be fined the sum of fifty pounds
current money for failing to deliver a
copy of a Bill in Equity agst. Elisha
Walden when he served him a Subpeena

For reasons appearing to the Court it is ordered that the Judgment
entered agst. the said deft. at the last term Nisi be remitted and that
the plt. pay the Costs of this motion.

Adjourned till court in course.

AUGUST TERM 1792

(p-33) At a Court of Equity begun and held in the town of Jonesborough
on the fifteenth day of August one thousand seven hundred and ninety two
for the District of Washington in the territory of the United States
South of the River Ohio.
            Present
                The Honourable
                        David Campbell)
                            &   ) Judges
                        Joseph Anderson)

Archibald Roan produced a commission in the words following (viz)
William Blount governor in and over the Territory of the United States of
America South of the River Ohio, To all who shall see these presents
Greetings, Know ye that I do appoint Archibald Roan of the County of
Greene, Clerk and Master in Equity for the District of Washington and
do authorize and empower him to execute and fulfil the duties of that
office according to law; and to have and to hold the said office of Clerk
and Master in Equity during his good behaviour, or the existence of the
temporary government of the said territory, with all the powers, privileges
and emoluments thereto of right appertaining.

Given under my hand and Seal in the said Territory this Seventh day
of March one thousand Seven hundred and ninety two (signed) William Blount.
By the Governor Dan Smith

With a Certificate thereon that he had taken an oath to support the
constitution of the United States and the Oath of Office.

(p-34) Archibald Roan entered into and acknowledged his Bond to the Judges
together with Francis A. Ramsey, William Cocke and Landon Carter his
Securities in the Sum of two thousand pounds, for the safe keeping the
Records and faithful performance of the duties of Clerk and Master in
Equity.

```
Charles Hays       -    complt.)
        agst.                )   Bill & Injunction
Samuel Harris      -    Deft. )
```

By consent of the parties and their counsel and on motion of the counsel for the complainant. It is ordered that the publication or testimony on the behalf of the complainant be prolonged till Wednesday evening the 21st Instant.

Friday the 23d August 1792

William Blevins & others   -   Complainant)
            vs   )   In Equity
John Shelby   -   Defendant)

August 23d, 24th and 25th the above cause came on to be heard before the Honble David Campbell and Joseph Anderson Esqrs Judges of said Court in the presence of counsel learned in the Law on both sides; the plaintiffs Bill and Defendants answer were read the facts ascertained by verdicts found on the Several issues directed were duly considered and the several paragraphs of Law and Arguments offered by counsel on both sides in Support of the Claims set forth in the bill and answer were heard and on debate investigation and bearing of the matter, it appearing to the court here that the plaintiffs have not Supported either an equitable or legal claim to the premises in dispute claimed in the said Bill, and the Defendant having Supported his equitable and legal claim set forth in his answer. It is thereupon considered by the court here and their Honours do order adjudge and decree that the complainants Bill be dismissed and that the Defendant John Shelby do recover against the said complainant his costs.

(p-35)   David McPeters and Charles McDowell   *   Complt.)
                      vs   )   Original Bill
         Alexr Outlaw and John Heritage   -   Deft.)

For reasons appearing to the Court it is ordered that this suit be continued till next term and that commissions be awarded the plaintiffs and Defendants to take the Depositions of their witnesses giving the adverse party legal notice of the time and place at executing the same which commissions shall be executed within 5 months at the Expiration of which time publication of Testimony shall pass.

William Blevins   -   Complt.)
            vs   )   Bill and Injunction
John Brown   -   Deft.)

August 23d, 24th and 25th the above cause came on to be heard before the Honourable David Campbell and Joseph Anderson Esquires Judges of said Court in presence of counsel learned in the Law on both sides. The plaintiffs Bill and the defendants answer were read, the facts ascertained by verdict found & were duly considered, and the Several paragraphs of Law and arguments offered by counsel on both sides in Support of the claims set forth in the bill and answer were heard; and on debate investigation and hearing of the matter, it appearing to the court here that the plaintiff hath not supported either, an equitable or legal claim to the premises in dispute claimed in the said Bill and the defendant having Supported his equitable and Legal claim set forth in his answer. It is thereupon considered by the Court here, and their Honours do order adjudge and Decree that the Complainants Injunction heretofore obtained against the Judgment of the said John Brown at Law be dissolved and that the complainants bill be dismissed and that the said Defendant recover against the said complainant his costs.

(p-36)   John Adair   )
                vs   )   Bill and Injunction
         Edmond Williams)

This cause came on to be heard this day and on hearing the Bill and
answer and proofs taken in the cause read, and hearing what was <u>alledged</u>
by the counsel on both sides; and because the court will advise thereon it
is continued till next term.

Jno Aaronwine   -   complt.)
                vs   )   Bill and Injunction
John Shelby   -   deft.)

For reasons appearing to the court it is ordered that this cause be
continued till next term and that publication be prolonged for 5 months.

Charles Hays   -   complt.)
                vs   )   Bill and Injunction
Samuel Harris   -   deft.)

For reasons appearing to the court it is ordered that this cause be
continued till next term and that publication of testimony be prolonged
and that a commission be awarded the complainant to take the Deposition
of Bates and Commissions to Defendent to take the depositions of Wm Sharpe
and Ezekiel Smith.

Henderson and Company)
                vs   )   Original Bill
Henderson and Company)

Some of the Heirs and Devisees having failed to enter their appearance
according to the Rules of this Court and it appearing to the Satisfaction of
the Court that they reside without the limits of this territory on the motion
of said complainants by their <u>attornies</u>, it is ordered   (p-37)   that unless the said Heirs and Devisees shall appear here on the first day of the
next term and answer the Bill of the complainant that then it shall be taken
for confessed and that a copy of this order be forthwith inserted in the
Kentucky Gazette and the newspaper regularly published in Hagerstown.

John Shelby   -   complt.   )
                vs   )   Instituted by consent to perpetuate
William Blevins and others - defts.)   Testimony

For reasons appearing to the court it is ordered that this cause be
dismissed at mutual costs.

Den on the Demise of   -   )
John Shelby   )   Ejectment instituted by consent
                vs   )
William Blevins and others -

For reasons appearing to the Court it is ordered that this case be
continued till next term.

George Martin   -   complt.)
       vs   )   Bill and Injunction
Andrew English   -   defendt.)

     For reasons appearing to the Court this cause is ordered to be con-
tinued till next term and that commissions be awarded to the parties to
take depositions of their witnesses and that publication of Testimony pass
at the Expiration of five months.

(p-38)   William Nelson   -   complt.)
              vs   )
       John Hannah   -   Deft.)

     For reasons appearing to the court it is ordered that this cause be
continued till next term and that commissions be awarded the parties to take
the depositions of their witnesses, which commissions shall be executed
in five months at the expiration of which it is ordered that publication of
Testimony do pass.

William Blevins   -   complainant)
         vs   )   Bill and Injunction
John Shelby   -   Defendant)

     August 23d, 24th and 25th this cause came on to be heard before the
Honble David Campbell and Joseph Anderson Esqrs. Judges of said Court in
the presence of counsel learned in the law on both sides, the plaintiffs
Bill and the defendants answer were read; the facts ascertained by verdicts
found on the several issues directed were duly considered and the several
paragraphs of law: and arguments offered by counsel on both sides in support
of the claims set forth in the Bill and answers were heard and on debate,
investigation and hearing of the matter, it appearing to the court here,
that the plaintiff hath not Supported either an equitable or legal title
or claim to the premises in dispute claimed in the said Bill   (p-39)   and
the Defendant having supported his equitable and legal claim and title set
forth in his answer: It is considered by the court here and their Honours
do order adjudge and decree that the complainants Injunction heretofore
obtained against the Judgment of the said John Shelby at law be dissolved
and that the complainants said Bill be dismissed and that the said John
Shelby defendant do recover against the said complainant his costs.

Alexander Hamilton   -   complainant)
            vs   )
James Patterson   -   Defendant)

     Ordered that a Scirefacias issue to the Executors or Administrators
of the Defendant to revive the proceedings in this cause.

Henry Massingale   -   complt.)
       vs   )   Original Bill
David Hughes and James Stuart - Defts.)

     By consent of the parties it is ordered that this cause be dismissed
and that the Defendant David Hughes pay his own costs and James Stuart
recover his costs.

John Waddell   -   complainant)
     vs   )   Bill and Injunction
Robert Patterson -   defendant)

      For reasons appearing to the Court it is ordered that this cause be continued till next term and that commissions issue to the parties to take the depositions of their witnesses.

(p-40)   William Cox   -   complainant)
                vs   )   Bill & Injunction
        Augustine Bromley - Defendant)

      Ordered that this cause be continued till next term and that commissions be awarded the parties to take the Depositions of their witnesses, which shall be executed within five months at the expiration of which time publication of the Testimony shall pass.

Peter McCall   -   complainant)
     vs   )   Original Bill
John Fegan   -   Defendant)

      For reasons appearing to the court it is ordered that the Rule of Reference heretofore made in this cause be set aside and that the Defendant put in his answer to the Bill.

Moses Humphreys   -   complainant)
        vs   )   Bill and Injunction
Matthew Talbot   -   Defendnat)

      On motion of the Defendant by his attorney (after reading the complainants Bill and the Answer of the Defendant and hearing the Arguments of Counsel on both sides) it is ordered by the Court that the complainants injunction heretofore obtained against the Judgment at Law of the Said Defendant be dissolved and that the Said Complainant pay the costs, in this behalf expended---- By consent of the said complainant it is further ordered that his Bill of   (p-41)   complainant be dismissed and that the Defendant Matthew Talbot do recover against the said complainant his cost.

George Mitchell   -   complt.   )
       vs   )   In Equity
John Carney   -   Defendant)

      By consent of the plaintiffs attorney it is ordered that this Suit be Dismissed.

William Ashert   -   complt.   )
      vs   )   Original Bill
John Cox Sen., John Cox Junr. and)
Thomas Amis   -   Defendants)

      The defendants having filed their several answers to the complainants bill, it is ordered that this cause be continued till next term and that commissions be awarded to the parties to take the depositions of their witnesses.

```
Samuel Wilson    -    complainant )
     vs                           )   Bill & Injunction
Elisha Wallen    -    defendant   )
```

The Defendant having filed his answer to the complainants bill It is ordered that this cause be continued till next term, and that commissions be awarded the parties to take the depositions of their witnesses.

```
(p-42)   Robert Kerr   -   complt. )
              vs                    )   Bill and Injunction
         Alexander Meek -   Deft.   )
```

The Defendant having filed his answer to the complainants bill It is ordered that this cause be continued till next term and that commissions issue to the parties to take the Depositions of their witnesses.

```
John Vance       -    complainant )
     vs                           )
John Laughlin &                   )   Original Bill
Robert Craig Exr  -  Defendants   )
of the Last Will and              )
Testament of John Laughlin Deceased)
```

```
Austin Shoat     -    complt.)
     vs                      )   Bill and Injunction
Ephraim Dunlop   -    Deft.  )
```

```
John Shirley     -    complt.)
     vs                      )   In Equity
John Gilliland   -    Deft.  )
```

For reasons appearing to the Court it is ordered that the Defendants in the foregoing Suits have time till the next term to plead Answer or Demur.

```
(p-43)   Samuel Smith - complt.    )
              vs                   )   In Equity
         Philip Saunders )Defendants )
         and Mary Saunders)
```

On motion of the attorney for the complainant and for reasons appearing to the Court it is ordered that the Rule, that the complainants bill be taken pro confesso entered at last term be set aside at the complainants costs and that a Subpoena Issue to the Defendants to put in their answer to the Complainants Bill.

```
John Tye         -    Complt.)
     vs                      )   Bill and Injunction
David Reese      -    Deft.  )
```

On motion of the complainants attorney it is ordered that a Subpena issue to Hawkins County, for the Defendant to put in his answer to the complainants bill.

```
David Boothe     -    complt.)
     vs                      )   In Equity
Benjamin Ford)   -    Defend.)
     vs
Garret Fitzgerald)
```

The Demurrer of the Defendants to the bill of the complainant being read and on argument of the counsel on both sides   (p-44)   It is ordered that the Demurrer of the Defendants be overruled and that they put in their answer to the complainants Bill.

Court adjourned till Court in Course.

FEBRUARY TERM 1793

(p-45)   At a Court of Equity begun and held at the Court house in Jones-borough for the District of Washington in the Territory of the United States of America South of the River Ohio on the fifteenth day of February one thousand Seven hundred and ninety three.
Present
The Honourable
David Campbell)
and   ) Judges
Joseph Anderson)

David McPeters and Charles McDowell)
vs   )
Alexander Outlaw John Heritage   )

By the consent of the parties and their attornies it is ordered that this cause be dismissed and that the costs be taxed according to a written agreement filed.

John Aaronwine   -   complainant)
vs   ) Bill and Injunction
John Shelby   -   Defendant)

By consent of both parties by their attornies it is ordered that this cause be continued till next term.

(p-46)   John Adair   - complt.)
vs   )   Bill and Injunction
Edmond Williams - Deft.)

This day came the parties by their attornies and thereupon also came a Jury (to wit George Doherty, Samuel Wilson, Nicholas Perkins, Thomas Henderson, Thomas Hutchings, John Patterson, John Shelby, James White, Asabel Rawlings, George McNutt, George Vincient, and David Caldwell who being duly sworn well and truly to enquire what damages Edmond Williams hath Sustained by reason of John Adair failing to send him certain proofs according to contract upon their oaths do say that they assess the damages substained by Edmond Williams by reason of the failure of John Adair to one hundred and thirty four pounds fifteen shillings.

Whereupon and on hearing the Bill and answer read and what could be alledged by the Counsel on both sides and on debate and Investigation of the Matter it is considered by the Court and their Honours do order adjudge and Decree that the Injunction for the sum of thirty four pounds Seventeen Shillings of the Judgment obtained by the said Edmond Williams at Law be made perpetual and that the injunction for the residue of the said Judgment, that is to say for the Sum of one hundred and thirty four pounds fifteen shillings be dissolved and that the said Edmond Williams have the Benefit of his Judgment at Law for the said Sum of one hundred and thirty four pounds fifteen Shillings (p-47) and the Court do further order and decree that the complainant and John Adair do recover against the said Edmond Williams his costs in this behalf expended.

Ordered that the foregoing decree be signed and enrolled.

Charles Hays   -   compl.   )
    vs   )   Bill and Injunction
Samuel Harris - Defendant)

Ordered by the Court with the assent of the parties that the following Issues of fact be tried by a Jury in this cause viz.
1st. Whether Aaron Burlison, Jesse Bounds, Stephen Harris, and Thomas Bates or some of them from whom Charles Hays the complainant derives his title had made any lawful Improvements on the premises in dispute before opening the Land office in the year 1778.

2nd. Whether Thomas Bates entered a claim for the premises in dispute, before the first day of January in the year 1779.

Whereupon came the parties by their attornies and also came a Jury Viz.

1. George Dougherty
2. Thomas Hutchings
3. John Patterson
4. John Nelson
5. George McNutt
6. George Vincient
7. David Caldwell
8. Anamias McCoy
9. Thomas Gilaspie
10. Adam Meek
11. Thomas Rodgers &
12. Archibald Blackburn

who being duly impannelled and Sworn to try the first issue before mentioned on their oaths do say (p-48) that Aaron Burlison, Jesse Bounds, Stephen Harris, Thomas Bates or some of them from whom Charles Hays the complainant derives his title made a Lawful improvement on the premises in dispute, before opening the Land office in the year 1778.

The Defendant Samuel Harris in open Court admits that Thomas Bates entered a claim for the premises in dispute before the first day of January in the year 1779.

This cause came on to be heard and the Bill and answer being read and the Arguments of Counsel on both sides heard and because the Court will advise thereon it is ordered to be continued till next term.

George Martin   - complt.)
    vs   )   Bill and Injunction
Andrew English -   Deft.)

William Box   -   Complt.)
    vs   )   Bill and Injunction
Augustine Bromley - Deft.)

By consent of the parties and their attornies it is ordered that the above causes be continued till next term.

William Nelson   -   Complt.)
    vs   ) Bill & Injunction
John Hannah   -   Deft.   )

This day came William Cocke attorney for the complainant and Dismissed
the Bill of the said William Nelson.

(p-49)   Henderson and Company)
                        vs   )   Original Bill
         Henderson and Company)

Some of the Heirs and Devisees having failed to enter their appearance
according to the Rules of this Court and it appearing to the Satisfaction of
this Court that they reside without the limits of this Territory on Motion
of the Said complainant by their attorney it is ordered that unless the said
Heirs and Devisees Shall appear here on the first day of the next term and
answer the Bill of the complainants that then it shall be taken pro confesso ;
and that a copy of this order be forthwith published for two weeks successively in some Gazette regularly published in the State of Maryland and in
the State of Kentucky.

Den on the Demise of John Shelby)
                        vs   )   Ejectment instituted by consent
William Blevins and others   )

For reasons appearing to the Court it is ordered that a Writ of possession issue to the Sheriff of Sullivan County to put John Shelby in
possession of the Premises in the Declaration of Ejectment Specified.

Alexander Hamilton - complt.)
                        vs   )   Original Bill
James Patterson   -   deft.)

John Scott Sheriff of Sullivan County made return that he had made
known the scire facias to the representatives of James Patterson Deceased
(p-50)   It is thereupon ordered by the Court that this suit be revived--
and on motion of the attorney for the Defendant it is ordered that a Scire
facias issue to the plaintiff to show cause why he should not give better
Security for the prosecution of his Bill of Complainant.

John Waddell   -   Complt.)
                        vs   )   Bill and Injunction
Robert Patterson -   Deft.)

William Ashert -   complt.)
         Cox vs   )
John/Senior)   .   )   Original Bill
John Cox Junr and) -Defts.)
Thomas Amis   )

For reasons appearing to the Court it is ordered that these causes
be continued till next term and that commissions issue to the parties to
take the depositions of their witnesses.

Peter McCall   -   Complt.)
                        vs   )   Original Bill
John Fegan   -   Deft.)

This cause is ordered to be continued till next term for the defendant
to put in his answer to the Complainants Bill.

(ø-51)   Samuel Wilson -   complt.)
             vs   )   Bill and Injunction
          Elisha Wallen -   Deft.)

This cause is ordered to be continued till next term and that commissions issue to the parties to take the Depositions of their witnesses which commissions shall be executed within six months at the expiration of which time publication of the testimony shall pass.

John Vance - Complt.)
         vs   )   Original Bill
John Laughlin and)- Deft.)
Robert Craig   )

The parties having Submitted to arbitration all the matters and things respecting this cause and the arbitration having returned their award to this Court it is ordered that the same be filed and confirmed.

Samuel Smith - Complt.)
        vs   )   Original Bill
Philip Saunders and) - Deft.)
Mary his wife   )

The Demurrer of the Defendants to the Bill of the complainant being heard and on argument of the council on both sides it is considered by the Court, that the said Defendants shall not be compelled to make any other answer to the said Bill and that the said Defendants recover their costs by them in this behalf expended.

(p-52)   William Cocke   -   Complt.)
              vs   )   Original Bill
          Richard Henderson)-- Deft.)
          and Company   )

It is ordered that this cause be continued till next term.

John Tye -   Complt.)
       vs   )   Bill and Injunction
David Reese -   Deft.)

The Defendant David Reese having failed to enter his appearance according to the Rules of this court, and it appearing to the Satisfaction of the Court that he is not an inhabitant of this Territory it is ordered that the said David Reese do appear at our next Superior Court of Equity to be held for the district of Washington at Jonesborough on the third Monday of September next and answer the Bill of the Complainant, otherwise it will be taken proconfesso, and the matter thereof decreed accordingly and that a copy of this order be inserted in the Knoxville Gazette.

(p-53)   David Boothe - Complt.)
             vs   )   Bill
          Benjamin Ford and)- Defts.)
          Garrett Fitzgerald)

The Defendants having filed their answers to the Bill of the Complainant It is ordered that Commissions issue to the parties to take the Depositions of their witnesses.

Austin Shoat   -   Complt.)
  vs   ) Injunction
Ephraim Dunlop -   Deft.)

   It is ordered with the consent of the parties by their <u>attornies</u> that
time of three months be given to the Defendant to put in his Answer, and
that commissions issue to the parties to examine their witnesses.

John Shirley - Complt.)
  vs   ) Bill
John Gilliland - Deft.)

Thomas Hutchings - Complt.)
  vs   ) Injunction
Henry Conway   - Deft.)

   For reasons appearing to the court it is ordered that the defendants
in these causes have time till next term to plead answer or Demur.

(p-54) William Gardiner   -   Complt.)
      vs   ) Bill
    Mary Looney and   -   Deft.)
    the Heirs of Benjamin Looney Decd.

   Time is given the Defendants till next term to put in their answer to
the Complainants Bill and it is ordered by the Court that Walter Johnston
be appointed Guardian for the Orphans of Benjamin Looney Deceased to Defend
this Suit on their behalf.

   Court adjourned till the third Monday of September next.

SEPTEMBER TERM 1793

(p-55) At a Court of Equity begun and held for the District of Washington
within the Territory of the United States of America South of the River Ohio
in the Court House of the County of Washington 25th day of September one
thousand Seven hundred and ninety three ------

Present
The Honble
David Campbell)
&   )   Esqrs.
Joseph Anderson)

   Landon Carter produced a commission which is in the words following
to wit. William Blount Governor in and over the Territory of the United States
of America South of the River Ohio; To all who shall see these presents
Greeting: Know ye that I do appoint Landon Carter Esqr. Clerk and Master in
Equity for the District of Washington to have and to hold the said office of
Clerk and Master in Equity for the District aforesaid with all powers
previleges and Emoluments there to belonging during his good behaviour or
<u>during his good</u> during the Existence of the temporary Government thereof

given under my hand and Seal at Knoxville in the Territory afóresaid this thirtyeth day of March one Thousand Seven Hundred and ninety Three Signed William Blount with a certificate (p-56) thereon that he had taken and Oath to Support the Constitution of the United States and the oath of office

John Aaronoen)
    vs   ) Bill & Injunction
John Shelby)

Ordered that the following Issue of Fact be tried in the above Cause, whether the Rights of Preoccupation to the Four Hundred acres of Land now in dispute be Vested in John Aaronoen by purchase from those under whom he claims or in John Shelby by purchase from those under whom he claims.

A Jury Impanneled and Sworn (to wit) Joseph Britten, James Sevier, Samuel Henley, Walter Johnson, John Melekin, John Blair, Thomas Vencent, Michael Rawlings, John Beard, John Wear of Washington Joel Gillenwaters and John Strain on their oaths say they find the Right of preoccupation to the Four Hundred Acres of Land in dispute to be vested in the plaintiff John Aaronoen by purchase from those under whom he claims.

John Aaronoen - Complt.)
    vs   ) Bill
John Shelby - Deft.) Injunction

Wednesday the 25th of September 1793 the above cause came on to be heard before the Honble (p-57) Joseph Anderson Esqr a Judge of the said Court in the presents of Councel Learned in the Law on both Sides the Plaintiffs Bill and defendants answer being read and the Facts ascertained by Verdict found on Issues directed to be tried having been duly weighed and consedered the Several paragraphs of Law and Arguments of Council offered on both sides in Support of the claims set forth in the Bill and Answer was heard and on mature deliberation thereupon, It is considered by the Court here that the said John Aaronwine the complainant hath Supported his Equitable claim to the premises in dispute as set forth in his Bill, and his Honour doth thereupón adjudge and /Decree that the said Injunction to the Judgment at Law of him the said John Shelby be and the same is hereby made absolute and perpetual and his Honour doth further oŕder adjudge and decree that the said Grant of the said John Shelby whereupon he Recovered at Law for so much thereof as fall within the Lines of the Said John Aaronwine's Land aforesaid, be and the Same is hereby annuled and made Void and of no Effect and that the said John Aaronwine Recover his costs Except his own attorneys Fee, and that the said John Shelby be liable to all the costs in the Court of Law in his Suit in Ejectment by the complainants Bill injoined.

Charles Hays - Complt.)
    vs   ) Bill & Injunction
Samuel Harris - Deft.)

(p-58) Wednesday the 25th of September 1793 the foregoing cause came in to be heard before the Honble Joseph Anderson Esqr a Judge of said Court, in the presence of Counsel learned in the Law ón both sides; the plaintiffs Bill and Defendants answer were Read and the Facts ascertained by verdicts found on the Issues directed to be tried, having been duely weighed & considered, the several paragraphs of Law and Arguments of Counsel offered on both sides, in Support of the claims set forth in the Bill and answer were heard; and on mature deliberation thereupon it is considered by the Court here that the said Charles Hays plt. hath Supported his equitable claim to the premises in dispute as set forth in his Bill, and his Honour doth thereupon adjudge and Decree that the said Injunction to the Judgment at Law of him the said Samuel Harris, be and the same is hereby made absolute and perpetual and his Honour doth further order adjudge and decree that the said Grant of him the said Samuel Harris whereupon he Recovered at Law for so much there of as falls within the Lines of the said Charles Hays's Land aforesaid, be and the same is hereby anmuled and made void, and of no Effect, and that the said Charles Hays recover his costs in this Honble Court and that the sd. Samuel Harris be liable for the costs at Law in his Suit by Ejectment by the complainants Bill enjoined.

(p-59) George Martin   -   Complt.)
            vs   )   Bill & Injunction
     Andrew English -   Deft.)

      This day came the parties by their <u>attornies</u> and thereupon came also a Jury to wit. Joseph Britain, John Wear of Green, Andrew Greer, James Sevier, Walter Johnson, Thomas Vencent, John Beard, John Wear of Washington, Joel Gillenwaters, John Melegin, Joseph Hardin, and Dillan Blevins, who being sworn well and truly to inquire whether Andrew English by himself or agent did take actual and peaceable possession of the Lands now in dispute and peaceably begin the first Improvement and carry on the same by <u>cuting</u> Logs for a House bringing the same together, and Raising the said House before the said George Martin came to take possession of the said Land; upon their oaths do say they find the Facts as stated in the above Issue in favour of the Defendant Andrew English.

      And the foregoing Jurors being sworn well and truly to inquire whether George Martin by himself or others availed himself of Force or threats to present said English's Improvement from being <u>compleated</u> as a Lawfull Improvement such as is now Required by Act of Assembly, upon their oaths do say they find in Favour of the defendants Andrew English.---

      And the aforesaid Jurors sworn well and truly to inquire whether the complainant George Martin directed or by his agent consented to any act which prevented Andrew English or his agent from <u>compleating</u> a Lawfull Improvement on the Lands in dispute as is Required by the Laws of North Carolina; upon their oaths say that George Martin did not direct or by his agent consent to any Act which prevented Andrew English or his Agent from <u>compleating</u> such lawfull Improvement on the Lands in dispute as is Required by the Laws of North Carolina.

(p-60) For reasons appearing to the Court it is ordered the foregoing cause be continued untill next term:

William Cox   -   Compt.)
     vs   )   Bill & Injunction
Augustine Brumley - Deft.)

      For reasons appearing to the Court it is ordered this cause be continued till the next Term and that Commissions Issue to take depositions in this Cause on giving legal notice of time and place of executing the same---

Henderson and Company - Complt.)
       vs   )   Original Bill
Henderson and Company - Deft.)

For reasons appearing to the Court it is orderthat this cause be continued till next term and Rule of publication Renewed.

Alexander Hamilton - complt.)
      vs   )   Original Bill
James Patterson - Deft.)

Sicri facias Returned not found by John McKay Deputy Sheriff Sullivan County; and on motion of the attorney for the defendant it is ordered that publication be made in the Noxville Gazette that the complainant appear at next term and shew cause why he should not give better Security for the prosecution of his Bill of complaint or else his Suit will be dismissed.

John Waddle - complt.)
   vs   ) Bill and Injunction
Robert Patterson - Deft.)

It appearing to the court that the Bail of the Defendant is insufficient and on motion of the attorney for the complainant it is ordered that unless the Defendant appear on the first day of the next Term and give better Security the Bill of complaint will be taken proconfesso and that a copy of this order be forthwith inserted in the Knoxville Gazette and that commissions be awarded to the complainant to take depositions of his witnesses.

(p-61) Peter McCall - complt.)
        John Fegan - Deft.) Original Bill

The defendant having filed his answer the first day of the Term, it is ordered that this cause be continued untill next Term and that commissions be awarded the parties to take the Depositions of their witnesses.

William Asherst - complt.)
      vs   ) Original Bill
John Cox Senr. John Cox Junr)-Deft.)
and Thomas Amis   )

For reasons appearing to the court it is ordered that this cause be continued untill next Term and that commissions Issue to the parties to take the depositions of their witnesses, directed to Colo. Henderson of Hawkins County to take the same.

Samuel Willson - complt.)
    vs   ) Original Bill
Elisha Wallen - Deft.)

For Reasons appearing to the Court it is ordered that this Cause be continued untill next Term and by consent of the parties no exception is to be taken in this cause before James White and Thomas Amis Esqrs. and that commissions be awarded to both parties to take the Depositions of their witnesses.

```
Robert Kerr     -     Complt.)
     vs                        ) Bill and Injunction
Alexander Meek  -     Deft. )
```

For reasons appearing to the court this cause continued & commissions awarded for both parties.

```
(p-62)   John Vance   -   complt.            )
              vs                             ) Original Bill
         John Laughlin, & Robert Craig - Deft. )
```

Ordered that the costs not provided for by the award filed be divided in proportion to the costs awarded.

```
William Cocke   -   complt.           )
     vs                               ) Original Bill
Richard Henderson & Company - Deft.)
```

For reasons appearing to the court this cause continued untill next Term.

```
John Tigh    -   complt.)
     vs                  ) Bill and Injunction
David Reese  -   deft. )
```

For Reasons appearing to the Court it is ordered that time be given the Defendant David Reese until next Term to put in his answer.

```
David Booth   -   complt.              )
     vs                                ) Original Bill
Benjamin Ford & Garret Fitzgerald - Defts.)
```

For reasons appearing to the Court it is ordered that this cause be continued untill next term and Rule for Publication at the end of Five Months and commissions awarded for both parties.

```
Auston Shoat   -   complt.)
     vs                    ) Bill and Injunction
Ephraim Dunlop -   Deft. )
```

Defendants answer filed the 13th of Aug. 1793 & the plaintiffs Exceptions filed 25th Sept. 1793- on motion of the plaintiff by his attorney it ordered that the defendant put in a more full and perfect answer within three months

```
(p-63)   John Shirley  -   complt.)
              vs                    ) Original Bill
         John Gillaland -   Deft. )
```

For reasons appearing to the Court it is ordered that this cause be continued untill next term and the defendant allowed a further time of Sixty Days to put in his answer.

```
Thomas Hutchings   -   complt.)
     vs                        ) Bill & Injunction
Henry Conway       -   deft. )
              Answer filed ---------------
```
On Reading Bill and answer it ordered that the Injunction be dissolved and the

Bill dismissed.

William Gardener - complt.)
      vs   )   Original Bill
Mary Looney & the Heirs of)- Defts.)
Benjamin Looney deceased)

Ordered by the Court that the Bill of the complainant be taken pro confesso
unless the answer of the defendant be filed within one hundred days.

Alexander McFarland - complt.)
      vs   ) Bill & Injunction
Robert Hood   - Deft.)

For reasons appearing to the Court it is ordered that Scira facias Issue to
the Executors or Administrators of the Defendant Robert Hood to Shew cause
why this Suit should not Revive.

(p-64)   John Carney - complt.)
              vs   )   Original Bill
       Ephraim Dunlop) - Defents)   :
            &   )
       Anne Moore   )

For Reasons appearing to the Court it is ordered that Ephraim Dunlop one of
the defendants put in a more full and perfect answer than the one filed by
the next Term also that publication be made in the Knoxville Gazett that
Anne Moore appear here at the next Term and put in her answer to the complainants Bill or else it will be taken for confesse as to her.

     Court adjourned untill the third Monday in March next.

                 MARCH TERM 1794

     At a Court of Equity begun and Held for the District of Washington
within the Territory of the United States of America South of the River
Ohio in the court house of the county of Washington the third Monday in
March 1794.

     Present
          The Hon. David Campbell)
                and   ) Esqrs.
            Joseph Anderson)

(p-65)   George Martin - complt.)
              vs   ) Bill & Injunction
       Andrew English - Deft.)

On motion of the Defendants attorney, It is ordered that a new Trial be granted
in the last Issue tried in this Suit at September Term 1793------
Whereupon there came a Jury impaneled tried and sworn (to wit) Thomas Hen-
derson, David Larken, John Jones, Nathaniel Davis, Benone Peremon, Robert
Allison, David Russell, Alex Greer, Leeroy Taylor, John Waddle and John
Beard, who upon their oaths say they find for the complainant George Martin

that he did not direct or by his agent consent to any thing that prevented Andrew English from making a Lawfull Improvement as is Reqd. by the laws of North Carolina on March 26th 1794, the foregoing cause came on to be heard before the Hon. David Campbell and Joseph Anderson Esqrs. Judges of Said Court in presents of Council Learned in the Law on both sides the plaintiffs Bill and Defendants answer being Red and the facts apportained by verdicts found on the Issues directed to be tryed. It is ordered by the court that the complainants Bill of Injunction be Dissolved.

```
William Cox    -   complt.)
      vs                  )   Bill & Injunction
Augustine Brumley - Deft. )
```

On motion of the Defendant by his attorney It is ordered that the Bill and Injunction of the complainant be dissolved.

```
(p-66)   Henderson and Company )
                 vs           )   Original Bill
         Henderson and Company )
```

For Reasons appearing to the Court, It is ordered that this cause be continued untill next Term and Rule for publication be Renewed in the Kentucky Gazett.

```
Alexander Hamilton  -  complt.)
       vs                     )   Original Bill
James Patterson     θ  Deft. )
```

```
John Waddle      -  complt.)
      vs                   )   Bill & Injunction
Robert Patterson -   Deft. )
```

For reasons appearing to the Court It is ordered that the foregoing causes be continued untill next Term and Rule for publication be enlarged untill next Term.

```
Peter McCall   -   complt. )
      vs                   )   Original Bill
John Feugan    -   Defendt.)
```

On motion of the Defendant by his attorney after reading the complainants Bill and Defendants Answer It is ordered that the Bill of the Complainant be dismissed.

```
(p-67)   William Asherst   -   compt.        )
                 vs                          )   Original Bill
         John Cox Sen. John Cox Jun.)-Defts.)
         and Thomas Amis             )
```

This cause dismissed by consent of plaintiff and Defendants they being present plaintiff paying his own attorneys Fee and the Defendants to be taxed with the Residue of the cost and this agreement to stand as a final Settlement between the parties to the present date.

Samuel Willson   -   compt.)
      vs   )   Bill & Injunction
Elishae Wallen   -   deft.)

For reasons appearing to the court it is ordered that this cause be continued untill next term and Rule for commissions for plaintiff.

William Cocke   -   compt.   )
      vs   )   Original Bill
Richard Henderson & Company - Deft.)

For reasons appearing to the court it is ordered that this cause be continued untill the next term.

John Tigh   -   compt.?
    vs   )   Bill & Injunction
David Rees.   -   Deft.)

For Reasons appearing to the court it is ordered that this cause be continued untill the next term and publication enlarged in the Knoxville Gazett.

(p-68)   David Booth   -   complt.   )
                vs   )   Original Bill
                Benjamin Ford and) - Defts.)
                Garret Fitzgerrald)

The foregoing cause came on to be heard before the Honourable David Campbell and Joseph Anderson Esqrs. Judges of the circuit aforesaid in presents of Council Learned in the Law on both sides the complainants Bill and the Defendants answers being Red It is ordered by the court that the complainants Bill be dismissed.

Auston Shoat   -   compt.)
      vs   )   Bill and Injunction
Ephraim Dunlop -   defendt.)

For reasons appearing to the court It is ordered that this cause be continued untill the next Term and Rule awarded for plaintiff and Defendant.

John Shirley   -   compt.)
      vs   )   Original Bill
John Gilliland -   defendt.)

The foregoing cause came on to be heard before the court in presents of Council Learned in the Law on both sides the complainants Bill and Defendants answer being Red. It is ordered that the Complainants Bill be Dismissed.

(p-69)   William Gardner - complainant   )
                vs   )   Original Bill
                Mary Looney and The Heirx)-Defendts.)
                of Benjamin Looney Deceased)

For reasons appearing to the Court It is ordered that this cause be continued untill next term and that Mary Looney answer with Four Months also

Rule for commissions for complainant and defendant.

Alexander McFarlan - compt.)
    vs   )   Bill & Injunction
Robert Hood   -   Deft.)

For reasons appearing to the court It is ordered that this cause be continued untill next Term and that James Richardson one of the defendants
put in an answer within three months also commissions awarded for complainant and defendant.

John Carney   -   compt.)
    vs   )   Bill & Injunction
Ephraim Dunlop and)- Defts.)
Anne Moore   )

For reasons appearing to the court it is ordered that this cause be continued untill next term and Rule of publication enlarged untill the next
Term.

(p-70)   Robert Keer   -   compt.)
          vs   )   Bill & Injunction
        Alexander Meek - Defendt.)

For reasons appearing to the court it is ordered that this cause be continued untill the next term and commissions awarded for complainant and
defendant.

William Blevins - compt.)
    vs.   )   Bill & Injunction
John Shelby   - Defendant)

On petition it is ordered that a new Trial be granted in this cause and
ordered by the Court that notice Issue to the Defendant.

Joseph Rannals - compt.   )
    vs   )   Original Bill
Ruth Tool Administrator   ) - Defts.)
      &   )
Archibald Roan and   )
John Hacket administrators)
of John Tool Deceased   )

For reasons appearing to the court it is ordered that this cause be continued untill next term and on motion it is further ordered that Archibald
Roan be appointed Guardian to this suit in behalf of the orphans.

(p-71)   John Gilliland - compt.)
          vs   )   Bill & Injunction
        John Shirley   - Deft.)

On motion it is ordered by the court that this Suit be continued untill the
next term and commissions to Issue for complainant and Defendant by consent.

```
John Hannah  -  compt.   )
        vs               )   Fi Fa
Charles Robinson         ))
        &                )
Jorden Roach Securities  )
for William Nelson       )
```

Fi Fa Executed on Charles Robinson and <u>Service</u> acknowledged also Executed
on Jorden Roach in presence of Thomas Berry & James Reed.

Geo Gillaspie, Shff.

It is ordered by the Court that Judgment be awarded against the Bail in this
Suit.

Court adjourned untill the third Monday in September next.

SEPTEMBER TERM 1794

(p-72) At a Court of Equity begun and held for the district of Washington
at the court house in Jonesborough on Tuesday the 16th of September 1794
Present the Honorable

```
                    David Campbell   )  Esqrs
                    John McNairy &   )  Judges of
                    Joseph Anderson )  Said Court
```

(Part of p-72 and p-73 faded out, impossible to read)

(p-73) North Carolina in the months of Jany. and October 1779 paid the
consideration to the State of North Carolina and made his Entries according
to law and afterwards obtained a grant thereupon. 4th. That the assembly
of North Carolina in the year 1782 passed a law, declaring the Grant under
which the Defendant claimed valid. 5th. The counsel for the plaintiff
Supposing that his first occupancy agreeable to the Laws of nature gave
him an Equitable title to the land which being afterwards confirmed by his
Entries and the Grant obtained from North Carolina for the same and supposing that the act of 1782 is a violation of the laws of contracts of
nature the unalienable rights of man and the constitution of the State;
In as much as the Legislature is passing the act aforesaid assumed a right
which was not nor could have been conceded by the said   (p-74)   constitution to wit. The disposition of private property and for the Effectual
prosecution of the aforesaid appeals the complainant William Blevins gave
Dellin Blevins and John Carter Securities who were bound in Eight Hundred
Dollars.

```
William Blevins and others  -  complt.)
              vs                       )
John Shelby                 -  Deft.   )

William Blevins   -   compt.)
      vs                    )
John Brown        -   Deft. )
```

On Rehearing the two last Suits it is ordered by the Court that the petition for Rehearing be set aside and the claim of the Defendants be confirmed and appeal prayed and Granted as in the foregoing Suit.

Charles Hayes   -   complt.)
             vs   ) Bill & Injunction
Samuel Harrison -   Deft.)

On petition of Samuel HarrisDefendant for a rehearing in this cause and order of Survey etc. and on argument and Reasons appearing to the Court ordered that a Rehearing of the aforesaid cause be had at the next Term and that in the mean time that the premises be surveyed and plotted according to an Entery made in the name of Thomas Batts and according to an Entery made in the name of Jesse Bean on which said Hayes Grant Issued and also according to the Lines of said ----- grant and plated in said manner as to shew how the Lines interfer and that Francis Alexander Ramsey execute the same.

(p-75)   Henderson and Company   - compt.)
                        vs   ) Original Bill
              Henderson and Company   - Defts.)

It appearing to the satisfaction of the Court that publication heretofore ordered have actually been made in this Suit agreeable been made in this Suit to such order in the publick Gazetts of Kentucky, Hagerstown, Knoxville & North Carolina and the Defendants having failed to put in there answers It is ordered that the Bill of the complainants be taken proconfesso and set for Tryal at next Term.

Alexander Hamilton   -   compt.)
             vs   )   Original Bill
James Patterson   -   Deft.)

On motion of the Counsel for the defendant It is ordered by the Court here that the Bill of the Complainant be dismissed he failing to enter Sufficient Security agreeable to the Rules and order of this Court at last term.

John Waddill   )
         vs   ) Bill and Injunction
Robert Patterson)

Agreeable to a Rule of this Court Robert King and James Hubbert came in and entered themselves Bail for the Deft. in five hundred dollars, and on motion it is ordered that copy of depositions of plaintiff and Defendant Issue for the Plaintiff, also Rule for commissions for plaintiff and Defendant and Rule for publication five months hence.

(p-76)   Samuel Willson - complt.)
                        vs   ) Bill and Injunction
              Elisha Wallen - Deft.)

    Publication being passed this cause came on to be heard the 27th of September 1794, and for Reasons appearing to the Court it is ordered to be continued untill next Term.

```
William Cocke    -   complt.)
         vs               )     Original Bill
Richard Henderson)- Defts. )
        &                 )
Company                   )
```

For reasons appearing to the Court it is ordered that this cause be continued.

```
John Tye        θ   Complt.)
         vs               )     Bill and Injunction
David Rees       -    Deft. )
```

It appearing to the court that the Defendant failed to put in his answer agreeable to the Rules thereof It is therefore ordered by the Court here that the complainants Bill be taken proconfesso and set for trial exparte.

```
Auston Shoat     -   compt. )
         vs               )     Bill & Injunction
Ephraim Dunlop   -    Deft. )
```

Commissions awarded for plaintiff and Defendant and for Reasons appearing to the Court it is ordered that this cause be continued.

```
(p-77)   William Gardner         )        )
             vs                  ) Complts.)   Bill & Injunction
         Mary Looney & the heirs of)      )
         Benjamin Looney Deceased )
```

For Reasons appearing to the Court it is ordered that the complainant have Leave to mend his Bill within three months, and the Defendants have untill next term to mend his answer.

```
Alexander McFarland   -   compt.)
         vs                     )  Bill & Injunction
Robert Hood           -    Deft.)
```

Rule for commissions for plaintiff and Defendant and publication five months hence.

                          MARCH TERM 1795

At a Court of Equity begun and held for the District of Washington at the Court house in Jonesborough on March 17th 1795.
```
                    Present the Honorable ) Esqrs.
                       David Campbell &    ) Judges of
                       Joseph Anderson     ) Said Court
```

```
William Blevins   -   complt.)
         vs                  )   Bill & Injunction
John Shelby       -    Deft. )
```

```
William Blevins)  -   complts.)
     & others  )              )
         vs    )              )
John Shelby       -    Defts. )
```

```
William Blevins   -   compt.)
      vs                     )
John Brown        -   Deft. )
```

In pursuance to a former Decree it is ordered by the court here that Executions Issue for costs in the foregoing Suits.

```
Den on the Demise of    )
John Shelby             )      Writ of Ejectment
      vs                )
William Blevins & others)
```

Agreeable to a former Decree it is ordered by the court that an alias Writ of possession Issue in favour of John Shelby.

```
(p-79)   Charles Hays   -   compt. )
              vs                   )   Bill & Injunction
         Samuel Harriss -   Deft.  )
```

On motion of the counsel for the Defendant it is ordered that order of Resurvey be Renewed and plats Returned to this Term and for Reasons appearing to the Court it is ordered that this cause be continued.

```
Henderson & Company   -   compts.)
      vs                         )   Original Bill
Henderson & Company   -   Defts. )
```

On the 17th day of March 1795 this cause came on to be heard the Defendants failing to put in their answer the complainants Bill being taken proconfesso at last Term and the aforesaid Bill being now Read it is ordered by the Court here that this cause be continued.

```
(p-80)   John Waddle  -  compt.  )
              vs                 )   Bill & Injunction
         Robert Patterson - Deft.)
```

The same day this cause came on to be heard and the death of defendant being Suggested, it is ordered by the court that Scire Facias Issue against the Executors or administrators to shew cause why the Injunction shall not be made perpetual.

```
Samuel Willson   -   compt.)
      vs               ·   ) Bill & Injunction
Elisha Wallen    -   Deft. )
```

The same day this cause came on to be heard and Reasons appearing to the Court on affidavit of the Defendant, It is ordered that this cause shall be open for the examination of Testamony on both sides for five months.

```
William Cocke     -   compt.)
      vs                    )   Original Bill
Richard Henderson) - Defts.)
& Company        )
```

For reasons appearing to the Court it is ordered that this cause be continued.

(p-81)   John Tye   -   compt.)
                  vs   )   Bill & Injunction
          David Rees   -.   Deft.)

The same day this cause came to be heard the complainants Bill being read
it is ordered by the court here that it be Rendered perpetual.

Auston Shoat   -   compt.)
         vs   )   Bill & Injunction
Ephraem Dunlop   -   Deft.)

The same day this cause came on to be heard and on motion it is ordered
that a Rule for publication of Testamony five months hence and commissions
awarded to take depositions for plaintiff and Defendant.

William Gardner   &   complt.   )
           vs   )   Original Bill
Mary Looney & the   ) - Defts.)
Eeirs of Benjamin Looney Decd.)

On motion it is ordered by the Court here that the Defendants have untill
next term to answer plead or demur.

(p-82)   Alexander McFarland - compt.)
                  vs   )   Bill & Injunction
          Robert Hood   - Deft.)

On March 28th 1795 this cause came on to be heard the plaintiffs Bill and
the Defendants Answer being read it is ordered by the Court here that the
plaintiffs Bill of Injunction be Dissolved & that the Respondents have the
Benefits of their Judgment at Common Law.

John Carney - compt.   )
     vs   )   Original Bill
Ephraem Dunlop &) - Defts.)
Ann Moore   )

For reasons appearing to the Court it is ordered that this cause abate as to
Ann Moore and on motion the plaintiff has leave to amend his Bill.

Robert Keer   -   compt.)
       vs   )   Bill & Injunction
Alexander Meek -   Deft.)

Joseph Rennalds - compt.   )   )
      vs   )   )   Original Bill
Ruth Tool Administratrix &   ) - Defts.)
Archibald Roan & John Hackett   )
Administrators of John Tool Decd.)

For reasons appearing to the Court it is ordered that the above cause be
·continued.

(p-83)   John Gilliland - compt.)
                  vs   )   Bill & Injunction
          John Shurley   - deft.)

On motion it is ordered by the Court here that a <u>Ducesteeum</u> on behalf of
the Defendant Issue to James Sevier Clerk of Washington County Court to
bring up the Records Respecting the caveats between the parties and it is
agreed to, by the parties that the Death of Either shall not abate this
suit and for Reasons appearing it is ordered that this cause be continued.

```
David Booth    -  compt.        )
      vs                        )   Original Bill
Benjamin Ford       ) - Defts. )
      &                         )
Garrett Fitzgarrald)
```

Commissions awarded for plaintiff & Defendant & For Reasons appearing
to the Court it is ordered that this cause be continued.

```
Laurence Kettenring  -  compt.)
      vs                       )   Original Bill
John Keywood        -  Deft. )
```

Commissions awarded for plaintiff and Defendant and for Reasons appearing
to the Court it is ordered that this cause be continued.

```
(p-84)   James Berry  -  compt. )
            vs                   )   Bill & Injunction
         Thomas Amis  -   Deft. )
```

Rule for publication five months hence, commissions awarded for plaintiff
and Defendant and for Reasons appearing to the Court it is ordered that
this cause be continued.

```
John Feagan    -    compt.           )
      vs                             )   Sci Fa
Saml Willson & Peter McNamee) - Defts. )
Securities for Peter McCall )
```

Scire Facias made known to Samuel Willson in Presence of James Williams and
William Berry by Thomas Berry Sheriff also made known to Peter McNamee in
presence of George Moore and Robert Guinn for Robert Houston Sheriff.

The defendants being called it is ordered adjudged and decreed that final
Judgment be Entered up against them.

```
(p-85)   Andrew Greer Senior  - compt.)
            vs                         )   Bill and Injunction
         Michael Montgomery   - Deft. )
```

On reading Bill and answer it is ordered by the Court here that the Injunction
of the Complainant be dissolved and Bill retained as an original Bill, on
the Defendant giving Sufficient Security to abide by and perform the final
Decree of the Court that shall be rendered thereon, and commissions awarded
for plaintiff and Defendant.

```
Martin Armstrong   -   compt.  )
      vs                       )   Bill and Injunction
Andrew Greer       - Defendant )
```

. On reading Bill and Answer it is ordered by the Court here that the Injunction of the complainant be dissolved, and on motion of the plaintiff's
attorney the Bill is retained as an original Bill.--Exceptions be taken to
the plaintiffs Security, it is further ordered that he give other and
better Security and that the Defendant give Security to abide by the decree
that shall be finally rendered thereon.

Cotteral Bailey)
    agt.   )   Bill and Injunction
Andrew Greer   )

On motion of the Defendants attorney it is ordered that the Plaintiffs Bill
of complaint be dissolved and on motion of plaintiffs attorney it is retained as an original Bill, and that the Defendant give Security to abide
by the decree that shall be finally rendered thereon.

SEPTEMBER TERM 1795

(p-86)   At a Court of Equity begun and held for the District of Washington
at the Court house in Jonesborough the third Tuesday in September 1795.
                        Present the Honorable
                             David Campbell   )   Esquires
                             Joseph Anderson &)   Judges of
                             John McNairy   ))   said Court

Charles Hayes)
    vs   )   Rehearing
Samuel Harriss)

On the 24th and 25th of September 1795 this cause came on to be heard, and
on reading bill and asnwer it is ordered adjudged and Decreed that the former
decree made in September 1793 be confirmed, and the court will advise as to
the costs and it is further ordered that a writ of possession issue to
Samuel Harriss agreeable to his recovery at common Law for one hundred and
eight acres of Land laying within the line of his patent grant and without
the lines of Charles Hayes's of four hundred acres of Land lying on Lick
Creek in Greene County.

(p-87)   Henderson and Company   )
             against   ) Original Bill
         Henderson and Company)

For reasons appearing to the court here it is ordered that this cause be
continued untill next Term.

John Waddill   )
    agt.   ) Bill & Injunction
Robert Patterson)

On motion it is ordered that this cause be continued and for reasons appearing
to the court it is also ordered that Scire Facias issue against the legal
Heirs and representatives of the said Robert Patterson to appear at the next
Term and revive.

Samuel Wilson   )
   agt.   )   Bill and Injunction
Elisha Wallen)

On the 24 of Sept. 1795 this cause came on to be heard and the following
issue being found between the parties under the direction of the court viz.
whether the lands claimed by Elisha Wallen by Virtue of his oldest improvement so as to cover or take in the lands claimed by Samuel Wilson and now
in dispute whereupon came the parties aforesaid by their attornies and
also a Jury Viz: 1. Charles McCrea 2. Joseph Brittain 3. John Sevier 4. Joseph
Crouch 5. John Strain 6. William Medlock 7. John Crinder 8. George Vincent
9. James Gaines 10. William Evans 11. Robert Rutledge 12. John Morriss
(p-88)   who being duely impanneled and sworn on their oath do say that the
Land claimed by Virtue of the eldest improvement, and as the same was
Surveyed and marked out by John Coulter does cover the Land claimed by
Damuel Wilson now in dispute.

William Cocke   )
   against   )   Original Bill
Richard Hendson & Co.)

     For reasons appearing to the court it is ordered that this cause be
continued.

Austin Shoat   )
   verses   )   Bill and Injunction
Ephraim Dunlop)

For reasons appearing to the court it is ordered that this cause be continued.

William Gardner   )
     vs   )   Original Bill
Mary Looney and the heirs of)
Benjamin Looney deceased   )

For reasons appearing to the court it is ordered that this cause be continued
and also commissions awarded for plaintiff and Defendant.

(p-89)   John Carney)
          vs   )   Original Bill
      Ephraim Dunlop)

Ordered by the court that Scire Facias Issue to the Legal Representatives of
Ann Moore to appear at next court to revive.

Robert Kerr   )
   against   )   Bill & Injunction
Alexander Meek)

This cause continued by consent and commissions awarded for the defendant.

Joseph Renolds   )
     vs   )   Original Bill
Ruth Tool administratrix &   )
Archibald Roane, and John Hacket)
administrators of John Tool Deceased)

On Reading Bill and answer it is ordered adjudged and decreed;that the Bill be dismissed at costs of Defendants.

(p-90)   John Gilleland)
              against   )   Bill and Injunction
         John Shurley   )

On the 26th of September 1795 this cause came on to be heard a Jury impaneled and Sworn Viz. Samuel Wilson, John Criner, John Sims, Elisha Wallen, William Medlock, George Vincent, James Gaines, William Evans, Robert Rutledge, John Morriss, Garret Fitzgerald and James Ryan, who being duly sworn to try the following issue of fact, whether John Gilleland or John Shurley or those under whom they claim made the first lawfull improvement on the premises, on their oaths do say that John Gilleland made the first lawful improvement on the premises in dispute. And an argument of Council in behalf of plaintiff and Defendant it is decreed by the Court here, that the Bill of the said complainant be made perpetual.

David Boothe   )
    agt.   )   Rehearing
Benjamin Ford &   )
Garret Fitzgerald   )

For reasons appearing to the court it is ordered that this cause be continued.

(p-91)   Laurence Kettering)
                vs   )   Original Bill
         John Cawood   )

   This Cause continued by consent.

James Berry   )
    vs   )   Bill and Injunction
Thomas Amis   )

This cause continued on affidavit of Defendant and commissions awarded for defendant.

Andrew Greer Senr.   )
       vs   )   Bill and Injunction
Michael Montgomery   )

For reasons appearing to the court, it is decreed that the defendant have the benefit of his Judgment at law, Bond and Security being given according to the directions of the court and that this cause be continued and commissions be awarded for plaintiff and Defendant.

Martin Armstrong   )
       vs   )   Bill and Injunction
Andrew Greer &   )
John Letten Jones   )

On motion of the attorney for Andrew Greer one of the Defendants in this suit, it is decreed that he have the benefit of his Judgment at Law, on his giving Bond and Security to abide by the decree that shall be finally rendered thereon and it is further ordered   (p-92)   that publication be made in the

Knoxville Gazette that John Letton Jones appear at next Term and file his answer.

```
Cotteral Bailey  )
      vs         )   Bill & Injunction
Andrew Greer     )
```

On motion of the plaintiffs attorney it is ordered that he have leave to amend his bill.

```
David Wright     )
      vs         )   Original Bill
Alexander Baine  )
```

Ordered that publication be made in the Knoxville Gazette that Alexander Baine the defendant, file his answer at next term, and it appearing to the Satisfaction of the court here that he is not an inhabitant of this Territory, it is ordered, that Colonel Andrew Lewis, Colo. William McClenihan and Colonel James Barnet or either of them (of the State of Virginia) be appointed commissions to take the answer of the said Alexander Baine.

```
Richard Woods    )
      vs         )   Bill and Injunction
Batt Wood        )
Thomas Wood &    )
Benjamin Gest    )
```

On motion of the plaintiffs attorney it is ordered that publication issue to Batt Woods and Thomas Woods to answer at next term otherwise the Bill will be taken pro confesso.

```
(p-93)  John Fagan    )
            vs        )   Bill and Injunction
        John Wood     )
        John Pritchet )
        Edmund Bean   )
```

On motion it is ordered that the Defendants have time untill next term to answer.

```
Ruth Brown       )
      vs         )   Bill and Injunction
John McDowell    )
```

Ordered that the defendant have leave untill next term to file his answer and do appoint James Greenlee and William Irwin to take his answer.

```
John Clower      )
      vs         )   Bill and Injunction
John Fegan       )
```

Ordered by the court with the consent of the parties that this suit be arbitraited by George Rutledge, John Scott, William McCormack and Hugh Montgomery, and in case any of the parties should refuse to serve as arbitrators, the persons that did choose them may call upon any others that they think proper to do the business, and them four to meet on the Second Thursday in

February at Blountville and if they cannot agree they are to choose an
umpire and their award to be a Rule.

(p-94)   Stockely Donelson   )
                    vs   )   Bill and Injunction
         Nathaniel Henderson)

On motion it is ordered that this cause be continued untill next term.

William Cobb   )
     vs   )   Original Bill
William Conway &   )
Jessee Evans   )

For reasons appearing to the Court it is ordered that the plaintiff have
leave to amend his bill, and that George Conway be made a defendant to this
to the complainants bill and it is also ordered that John and Robert Adams
of the State of Virginia be appointed to take the answer of Jessee Evans.

John Gilleland   )
     vs   )   Scire Facias
James Stinson &   )
William Cox bail for   )
John Shurley   )

It is ordered by the court here that Execution issue against the Defendants
according to Scire Facias.

(p-95)   Andrew English   )
                   vs   )   Scire Facias
         Azariah Doty   )
         Bail for George Martin)

It is ordered by the court here that execution issue against the defenants
according to Scire facias.

MARCH TERM 1796

     At a Court of Equity begun and held in the Town of Jonesborough on
Friday the eighteenth day of March one thousand Seven hundred and ninety
Six for the District of Washington in the Territory of the United States of
America South of the River Ohio.
                        Present the Honable
                        Joseph Anderson Judge of
                              said Court

Charles Hays   )
     vs   )   Rehearing
Samuel Harriss   )

For reasons appearing to the court it is ordered that this cause be continued on the same Rule made at last Term.

Henderson & Co.)
   agt.)
Henderson & Co.)
   continued

John Waddell)   (Scre facias make known
   vs)   to William Patterson in the
Robert Patterson)   presence of Thos. Henderson and
                     John Mumpower. Thos. Berry Shff.)

Samuel Wilson)
   against)   Bill and Injunction
Elisha Wallen)

William Cocke)
   vs.)   Original Bill
Richard Henderson & Co)

For reasons appearing to the Court it is ordered that the foregoing causes
be continued.

Austin Choat)
   vs)   Bill & Injunction
Ephraim Dunlop)

Ordered by the Court that this cause be continued and that commissions be
awarded for the Defendant.

(p-97)   William Gardner)
          vs)   Original Bill
          Mary Looney)
          and the Heirs of)
          Benjamin Looney deceased)

Ordered by the court that this cause be continued and that commissions be
awarded for the plaintiff and defendant.

John Carney)
   vs)   Original Bill
Ephraim Dunlop)
and the legal Re-)
presentatives of Anne)
Moore deceased)
On motion of the plaintiffs attorney it is ordered by the Court here that
publication be made in the Knoxville Gazette for three months to the legal
representatives of Ann Moore to appear at next term and revive, otherwise
the Bill will be taken pro confessæ and publication the first day of next
Term also rule for commissions for plaintiff and _defenant._

Robert Kerr)
   agt.)   Bill and Injunction
Alexander Meek)

For reason appearing to the court it is ordered that this cause be continued
and commissions awarded for defendant.

(p-98)
David Boothe   )
    vs   )   Rehearing
Benjamin Ford &   )
Garret Fitzgerald

For reasons appearing to the court it is ordered that this cause be continued.

Laurence Kettering)
     vs   )   Original Bill
John Cawood   )

For reasons appearing to the court it is decreed that the plaintiff proceed within two terms, otherwise the suit will be discontinued rule for commissions for plaintiff and defendant.

James Berry   )
   vs   )   Bill and Injunction
Thomas Amis   )

For reasons appearing to the court it is ordered that this cause be continued commissions awarded for plaintiff & defendant.

Andrew Greer Senr.)
    vs   )   Bill and Injunction
Michael Montgomery)

For reasons appearing to the court, it is ordered that this cause be continued and that commissions be awarded for plaintiff & defendant also thirty days notice to the defendants attorney to take Testimony.

(p-99)   Martin Armstrong)
             vs   )   Bill & Injunction
        Andrew Greer &   )
        John Letten Jones)

For reasons appearing to the court it is ordered that this cause be continued and that commissions be awarded for plaintiff and Defendant, and it is also ordered that the plaintiff do proceed within two terms otherwise his bill be dismissed.

Cotteral Bailey   )
    vs   )   Bill and Injunction
Andrew Greer   )

On motion of the defendants attorney it is ordered that he have further time untill next term to answer the amended bill.

David Wright   )
    agt.   )   Original Bill
Alexander Baine)

On motion it is ordered by the court here that the defendant have further time, untill next term to file his answer.

(p-100) Richard Woods)
   vs)
  Batt Wood)   Bill and Injunction
  Thomas Wood &)
  Benjamin Gest)

It is ordered by the Court here that Benjamin Gest file his answer the first day of next term otherwise the bill will be taken confessed as to him, and that publication be made in three Successive numbers of the Knoxville Gazette that Batt Wood and Thomas Wood appear at the next term and file their answer otherwise the bill will be taken as confess'd.

John Fegan)
  vs)   Bill & Injunction
John Wood)
John Pritchet &)
Edmond Bean)

It appearing to the Court here that the Injunction was prayed to stay the costs of the complainants own Suit at law it is therefore ordered that the Injunction be dissolved so far as it respects the costs in the court below, but that the bill be retained as an original.

(p-101) Ruth Brown)
   vs)   Bill & Injunction
  John McDowell)

For reasons appearing to the Court, it is ordered that this cause be continued and that commissions awarded for plaintiff and defendant.

John Clower)
  vs)   Bill and Injunction
John Fegan)

(p-102) Stockley Donelson)
    vs)   Bill and Injunction
  Nathaniel Henderson)

It is ordered adjudged and decreed by the Court here that the plaintiffs bill of complaint be dissolved and that the defendant have the benefit of his Judgment at law.

William Cobb)
  vs)   Original Bill
William Conway and others)

It is ordered by the court that the defendants have further time untill next term to file their answer.

Stockley Donelson)
  vs)   Bill and Injunction
John Sheilds)

It is ordered that the defendant appear on the first day of the next term and file his answer.

Michael Harrisson	)	
vs	)	Bill & Injunction
William Murphy &	)	
Isaac Thomas	)	

Ordered by the Court here that James Greenlee (p-103) William Irwin and John Henry Stavelie Esquires and each of them be impowered by commission to take the defendants answer and it is further ordered by his Honor that the complainant give a better prosecution bond for the payment of the said Myrphys Judgment at Law as well as the costs of this Suit in case he fail herein otherwise the bill shall be dismissed at the next term.

SEPTEMBER TERM 1796

At a Court of Equity begun and held in the Town of Jonesborough on Friday the thirtyeth day of September one thousand Seven hundred and ninety Six for the District of Washington in the State of Tennessee.

Present the Honorable
John McNairy
Archibald Roane &
William Charles Cole Claiborn
Judges of Said Court

Charles Hayes	)	
vs	)	Rehearing
Samuel Harriss	)	

Ordered that this cause be continued and that the Court will advise as to the Costs.

(p-104) Henderson and Company	)	
vs	)	Original Bill
Henderson and Company	)	

John Waddill	)	
vs	)	Bill and Injunction
Robert Patterson	)	

Ordered by the Court that the foregoing Causes be continued.

Samuel Willson	)	
vs	)	Bill and Injunction
Elisha Wallen	)	

The foregoing cause compromised by the complainant and defendant (to wit) the defendant relinquishes to the complainant the land in dispute and gives up the said Land on the first day of January next and pay all costs except the complainants attorney and the attendance of the following witnesses (to wit) John Adair, Joseph Bishop, John Rice, John Wallen and James Anderson which was made a rule of this Court and cause ordered to be dismissed accordingly.

William Cocke	)	
vs	)	Original Bill
Richard Henderson and Company	)	

Ordered by the Court that Writ of Subpoena Issue to the defendants to answer the Amendments of the Complainants Bill.

(p-105) Auston Shoat   )
                vs   )   Bill and Injunction
         Ephraim Dunlop   )

Ordered by the Court that this cause be continued and that commissions Issue
to ------- Plaintiff and defendant.

William Gardner   )
        vs   )   Original Bill
Mary Looney and the heirs of   )
Benjamin Looney deceased   )

Ordered by the Court that a copy of the amended Bill of the complainant and
Writ of Subpoena Issue to the defendants to appear at next Term and answer

John Carney   )
        vs   )   Original Bill
Ephraim Dunlop &   )
the heirs of Ann Moore deceased   )

Ordered by the Court that this cause be continued and that commissions Issue
to plaintiff and defendant.
Robert Keer vs. Alexander Meek) Bill and Injunction
David Boothe   )
        vs   )   Rehearing
Benjamin Ford and   )
Garret Fitzgerrald   )

Ordered by the Court that the foregoing cause be continued.

(p-106) Lawrence Kettron   )
                vs   )   Original Bill
         John Keywood   )

On the thirtyeth of September 1796 this cause came on to be heard and there
upon also came a Jury (to wit) David Russell John Waddle, Alexander Nelson,
George Nowland, Robert Campbell, James Haywood, Walter Johnston, Alexander
Greer, Andrew Greer, David Kincade, Joseph Young and John Weir who being
sworn well and truly to inquire whether the premises claimed by the defendant
answer and contained within the lines of the grant to John Shelton under
which the defendant claims on their oaths do find that the premises claimed
by the defendants answer are contained within the lines of the grant to
John Shelton.

James Berry   )
        vs   )   Bill and Injunction
Thomas Amis   )

For reasons appearing to the court it is ordered that this cause be continued
and that commissions Issue to the Defendant.

Andrew Greer Senr.   )
        vs   )   Bill and Injunction
Michael Montgomery   )

Ordered by the Court that this cause be continued and that commissions
Issue to plaintiff and defendant.

(p-107)   Martin Armstrong   )
                    vs   )   Bill and Injunction
        Andrew Greer and   )
        John Letten Jones)

Ordered by the Court that this cause be continued.

Cottrd Bailey   )
    vs   )   Bill and Injunction
Andrew Greer Senr.   )

The defendant consents to a rule for commissions on condition that it shall
not preclude him from any advantage the pleadings or future progress of the
suit, and it is ordered by the court that their saving of advantage shall
be mutual.

David Wright   )
    vs   )   Original Bill
Alexander Bain   )

The plaintiffs death Suggested It is ordered by the Court that Scirefacias
Issue to the heirs of the said Alexander Bain to appear at the next Term,
and revive.

Richard Woods   )
    vs   )   Bill & Injunction
Batt Wood, Thomas Wood &)
Benjamin Gist   )

For reasons appearing to the court it is ordered that Batt Wood and Thomas
Wood have further time untill next term to file their answer.

(p-108)   John Fegan   )
                  vs   )   Bill & Injunction
        John Wood, John Pritchett &)
        Edmond Beans   )

Ordered by the court that John Wood and John Pritchett file their answer at
the next term other wise the plaintiffs Bill will be taken as confessed.

Ruth Brown   )
    vs   )   Bill & Injunction
John McDowell   )

Ordered by the Court that this cause be continued and that commissions Issue
to plaintiff and defendant.

William Cobb   )
    vs   )   Bill & Injunction
William Conway & others)

John Rhea attorney for the Defendants agrees to bring in the answer of
George Conway at next term on his receiving a copy of the order making of
the said George a party to the complainants Bill.

Michael Harrison)
    vs)   Bill & Injunction
William Murphy &)
Isaac Thomas)

On reading Bill and answer It is ordered adjudged and decreed that the
plaintiffs Bill be Dissolved and on-motion of the plaintiffs attorney It is
ordered that the Bill be retained as an Original and that copy of this decree
shall not Issue to Clerk at Law untill the said   (p-109)   William Murphy
shall give bond with Sufficient Security with condition that in case a decree be made in this Court against the said William Murphy that he shall
refund and pay back all sums recovered at Law and Such further sums as shall
or may be decreed for costs against him on a final determination of this
Suit.

Stockley Donelson)
    vs)   Bill and Injunction
John Shields)

Ordered by the Court that this cause be continued.

William Evans)
    vs)   Original Bill
Nathaniel Davis &)
James Charters)

Ordered by the court that this cause be continued.

Samuel May Senr.)
    vs)   Original Bill
George Ingle, Henry Oldham &)
Nancy Oldham)

For reasons appearing to the Court It is ordered that unless Nancy Oldham
by guardian appear at the next term and file her answer that the complainants
bill be taken as confessed as to her self and It is also further ordered that
alias Subpoena Issue to the other defendants to appear and file their answers.

(p-110)   John Sharp)
            vs)   Bill & Injunction
       John Adair)

Ordered by the Court that this cause be continued.

Edward Erwine)
    vs)   Original Bill
Benjamin Erwine)

For reasons appearing to the court It is ordered that the defendant have
further time untill next Term to file his answer.

On the first day of October 1796:
                                Present the Honorable John McNairy,
Archibald Roane and William Charles Cole Claiborn Judges of the Court of
Equity for Washington District in the State of Tennessee, when John Carter

was duly and constitutionally appointed Clerk and Master of said Court, and took the Several oaths, required Law and was commissioned as follows State of Tennessee Washington District September 1796. Pursuant to the authority vested in us by the constitution, (p-111) we have nominated and appointed John Carter Clerk and Master in Equity for the District aforesaid during his good Behaviour given under our hands the 1st day of October in the year 1796.

> John McNairy
> Archibald Roane
> William Charles Cole Claiborne

MARCH TERM 1797

At a Court of Equity begun and held for the District of Washington in the Town of Jonesborough on the 31st day of March 1797.
Present the Honorable
Archibald Roane and
William Charles Cole Claiborne
Judges of said Court.

Charles Hayes	)	
vs	)	Rehearing
Samuel Harris	)	

For reasons appearing to the court here it is decreed by their honors that Charles Hayes pay the costs of the rehearing.

(p-112) Henderson & Co.	)	
vs	)	Original
Henderson & Co.	)	

For reasons appearing to the Court It is ordered that this cause be continued

John Waddell	)	
vs	)	Bill & Injunction
Robert Patterson	)	

For reasons appearing to the court it is ordered that this cause be continued and publication of Testamony after five months

William Cocke	)	
vs	)	Original Bill
Richard Henderson & Co.	)	

It appearing to the court that the Several defendants contained the complainants Bill of complaint have not filed their answers It is therefore order by their honors that publication be inserted in the Knoxville Gazette and also in the Gazette published by Hodge and Willis at Halifax North Carolina for three weeks Successively that the several defendants appear at the next Term and file their answers otherwise the complainants Bill will be taken pro confesso.

(p-113) Austin Shoat	)	
vs	)	Bill of Injunction
Ephraim Dunlop	)	

For reasons appearing to the Court it is ordered that this cause be continued and publication of testimony after five months.

William Gardener   )   Original Bill
    vs   )
Mary Looney and the heirs)
of Ben Looney decd.   )

For reasons appearing to the Court it is ordered that this cause be continued and that commissions issue to plaintiff and defendant.

    On motion of the complainants attorney, and reason shewn, it is also ordered that the complainant have leave to withdraw the depositions by him filed.

John Carney
    vs
Ephraim Dunlop and the heirs of Ann Moore

For reasons appearing to the court it is ordered that this cause be continued and that commissions issue to plaintiff & defendant publication of testimony after five months.

(p-114)   Robert Keer   )
           vs   )   Bill & Injunction
       Alexander Meek)

For reasons appearing to the Court it is ordered that this cause be continued and commissions issue to plaintiff and defendant publication five months hence.

David Boothe   )
    vs   )   Rehearing
Benjamin Ford and Garet Fitzgerald)

For reasons appearing to the Court it is ordered that this cause be continued

Laurence Kettron   )
    vs   )   Original Bill
John Heywood   )

For reasons appearing to the Court it is ordered that this cause be continued and commissions issue to plaintiff and defendant publication after five months

James Berry   )
    vs   )   Bill & Injunction
Thomas Amis   )

For reasons appearing to the Court it is ordered that the complainant   (p-115) and Defendant have leave to amend Bill and answer. The complainant waves the privelege of amendment.

Andrew Greer Sen.   )
    vs   )   Bill & Injunction
Michael Montgomery   )

For reasons appearing to the Court it is ordered that publication of
Testimony be made on the fifth day of next Term unless cause be shewn
to enlarge the rule and that commissions issue to plaintiff and defendant.

Martin Armstrong)
     vs)   Bill & Injunction
Andrew Greer & John Letten Jones)

On motion of the defendant Andrew Greer's attorney it is ordered by the
Court here, that this cause be dismissed for the want of prosecution as required by an order made in March Term 1796.

Cotteral Bailey)
     vs)   Bill and Injunction
Andrew Greer)

Refered by consent of plaintiff and Defendant as appears by written agreement filed.

(p-116)   David Wright)
             vs)   Original Bill
        Alexander Bain)

On motion of the defendans attorney it is ordered by the court here, that
the complainant or his representatives appear at next Term and prosecute
this suit otherwise it will be dismissed.

Richard Woods)
     vs)   Bill & Injunction
Batt Wood, Thos. Wood & Ben Gest)

For reasons appearing to the Court it is ordered that Batt Wood have time
untill next Term to file his answer.

John Fegan)
     vs)   Bill & Injunction
John Wood, John Prichett &)
Edmond Been)

Dismissed by consent of parties and John Wood assumes the costs.

Ruth Brown)
     vs)   Bill and Injunction
John McDowell)

The Defendants death suggested, ordered by the Court that this cause be
continued.

(p-117)   William Cobb)
             vs)   Original Bill
        William Conway & others)

Ordered by Court that this cause be continued and that commissions issue to
plaintiff and Defendant.

Michael Harrison)
vs) Bill & Injunction
William Murphy and)
Isaac Thomas)

It is ordered by the Court that this cause be continued.

Stockley Donalson)
vs) Bill & Injunction
John Shields)

Ordered by the Court that this cause be continued.

William Evans)
vs) Original Bill
Nathaniel Davis &)
James Charters Exrs.)

Ordered by the Court that cause be continued.

(p-118)   Samuel May Senr.)
vs) Original Bill
George Ingle, Henry Oldham)
& Nancy Oldham)

For reasons appearing to the Court it is ordered that the other defendants
have further time to file their answers.

John Sharp)
vs) Bill and Injunction
John Adair)

Ordered by the Court to be continued.

Edward Erwin)
vs) Original Bill
Benjamine Erwin)

It is ordered by the Court that this cause be continued and that commissions
issue to plaintiff & defendant.

John Blevins)
vs) Bill & Injunction
John Shelby Senr.)

On motion of the complainants attorney it is ordered by the Court that he
have leave to amend his Bill and that commissions issue to plaintiff and
Defendant.

(p-119)   John Allison & others)
vs) Original Bill
Robert Allison & Francis Hodge)

Ordered that this cause be continued and that commissions issue for plaintiff
and defendant.

Ordered that this cause be continued and that commissions issue for plaintiff and defendant.

John Laughlin & Robt. Craig	)	
vs	)	Original Bill
John Vance	)	

It is ordered by the Court that unless the defendant appear at next Term and file his answer the Bill of the complainants will be taken pro confesso.

SEPTEMBER TERM 1797

At a Court of Equity begun and held for the district of Washington in the town of Jonesborough, on the 29th day of September 1797.

Present the Honorable   Esqrs.
Archibald Roan   )   Judges
William Charles Cole Claiborne &)   of said
Howel Tatham   )   Court

(p-120)   Henderson & Co.)
      vs   )   Original Bill
     Henderson & Co.)

John Waddell)
   vs)   Bill & Injunction
Robert Paterson)

William Cocke)
   vs)   Original Bill
Richard Henderson & Co.)

Austin Shoat)
   vs)   Bill & Injunction
Ephraim Dunlop)

For reasons appearing to the Court it is ordered that the foregoing causes be continued.

William Gardner)
   vs)   Original Bill
Mary Looney & the Heirs)
of Benjamin Looney Decd.)

It is ordered by the Court that this cause be continued and commissions issue for the plaintiff and defendant.

(p-121)   John Carney   )
      vs   )   Original Bill
    Ephraim Dunlop &)
    the Heirs of Ann Moore Decd.)

Robert Keer)
   vs)   Bill & Injunction
Alexander Meek)

David Boothe)
    vs)   Rehearing
Benjamin Ford &)
Garret Fitzgerald)

Ordered by the Court that the foregoing cause be continued.

Laurence Kettron)   Original Bill
    vs)
John Heywood)

It is ordered by the Court to be continued and commissions to issue to the
plaintiff & defendant.

James Berry)
    vs)   Bill & Injunction
Thomas Amis)

Ordered by the Court to be continued.

(p-122)   Andrew Greer Senr.)
             vs)   Bill & Injunction
       Michael Montgomery)

Cotteral Bailey)
    vs)   Original Bill
Andrew Greer Senr.)

For reasons appearing to the court it is ordered that the foregoing causes
be continued and that commissions issue for plaintiff and Defendant.

David Wright)
    vs)   Original Bill
Alexander Bain)

It is ordered by the Court that this cause be continued.

Richard Woods)
    vs)   Bill & Injunction
Batt Wood, Thomas Wood)
& Benjamin Gest)

On argument of Counsel for plaintiff and Defendant It is ordered adjudged and
Decreed by the court that the complainants Bill of complaint be taken pro
confesso as to Batt Wood.

(p-123)   Ruth Brown)
           vs)   Bill and Injunction
       John McDowell)

For reasons appearing to the Court here it is ordered that Scirefacias issue
against Ann McDowell widow Colonel John Carson & William Whitson Executors
of said John McDowell deceased to appear at the next term and revive.

William Cobb)
    vs)   Original Bill
William Conway & others)

For reasons appearing to the Court it is ordered that the plaintiff and defendant have leave untill next Term to amend Bill and answer, and that commissions issue to plaintiff & defendant.

Michael Harrison)
     vs)   Bill & Injunction
William Murphy &)
Isaa Thomas)

Stockley Donalson)
    vs)   Bill & Injunction
John Shields)

Williams Evans)
    vs)   Original Bill
Nathaniel Davis &)
James Charters)

(p-124)   Samuel May Senr.)
         vs)   Original Bill
      George Ingle, Henry Oldham)
      & Nancy Oldham)

Edward Erwine)
    vs)   Original Bill
Benjamin Erwine)

For reasons appearing to the Court it is ordered that the five foregoing causes be continued untill next Term.

John Sharp)
    vs)   Retained as an
John Adair)   Original Bill

On argument of counsel for plaintiff and Defendant, it is ordered adjudged and decreed by the Court here that the complainants Bill of Injunction be Dissolved and an argument of complainants attorney it is also ordered that his bill be retained as an original.

John Blevins)
    vs)   Bill and Injunction
John Shelby)

It is ordered by the Court that this cause be continued.

(p-125)   John Allison & others)
         vs)   Original Bill
      Robert Allison & Francis Hodge)

On the 26th of September 1797 this cause was compromised by the parties of mutual costs, which was ordered by the court to be entered of Record.

John Laughlin &)
Robert Craig)
    vs)   Original Bill
John Vance)

It is ordered by the Court that this cause be continued untill next Term.

John Johnson	)	
vs	)	Bill and Injunction
Moses Carrick	)	

It is ordered by Court that this cause be continued, and that commissions issue to plaintiff and Defendant.

John Willson	)	
vs	)	Original Bill
Andrew & Jacob Emmert	)	Compromised by the parties the plt.

pays his own attorney and all other costs except one half of the Sheriffs fee and half of the copying of the Bill the Balance assumed by Henry Harklerrode whig was ordered to be made a rule of this Court.

(p-126)

MARCH TERM 1798

At a Court of Equity begun and held for the District of Washington in the town of Jonesborough on the 15th day of March 1798.
Present the Honorable
Archibald Roan) Esqrs.
Howell Tatham) Judges of said
David Campbell) Court

Henderson & Co.	)	
vs	)	Original Bill
Henderson & Co.	)	

For reasons appearing to the court it is ordered that this cause be continued.

John Waddell	)	
vs	)	Bill & Injunction
Robert Patterson	)	

For reasons appearing to the court it is ordered that this cause be continued and set for trial at next Term.

William Cocke	)	
vs	)	Original Bill
Richard Henderson & Co.	)	

It is ordered by the Court that publication be made in the Knoxville, Lexington and Salisbury Gazettes; for the defendants to appear at next Term and file their answer otherwise the complainant's Bill will be taken pro confesso.

(p-127) Austin Shoat	)	
vs	)	Bill & Injunction
Ephraim Dunlop	)	

For reasons appearing to the Court it is ordered that this cause be continued & set for trial at next Term. Publication of Testimony after five months and that commissions issue for plaintiff and defendant.

William Gardner   )
  vs   )   Original Bill
Mary Looney and the   )
heirs of Benjamin Looney decd.)

For reasons appearing to the court it is ordered that this cause be continued
and commissions issue to plaintiff and Defendant. Publication of Testamony
on the first Monday of August next.

John Carney   )
  vs   )   Original Bill
Ephraim Dunlop   )

For reasons appearing to the Court it is ordered that this cause be continued
and that publication be made in the Knoxville Gazette that the heirs of
Ann Moore appear at the next term and file their answers otherwise the compt.
bill will be taken pro confesso also commissions issue to plaintiff and
Defendant.

(p-128) Robert Keer)
     vs   ) Bill and Injunction
   Alexander Meek)
      by
It is ordered/the Court that this caus be continued untill next term and
that commissions issue for plaintiff and Defendant.

David Boothe   )
  vs   )   Rehearing
Benjamin Ford and   )
Garret Fitzgerrald   )

On reading Bill and Answer and reasons shewn it is ordered by the Court that
the issues of facts filed by the Defendants be tried at the next Term, and
that commissions issue for plaintiff and Defendant.

Laurence Kettron   )
  vs   )   Original Bill
John Keywood   )

On argument of counsel for plaintiff and Defendant, it is ordered by the
Court here, that the Demurer be so far Sustained that the defendant shall
not be compelled to answer those parts of the complainants Bill that State
the complainants entering Claims in the entry office prosecuting caveats
against the defendant orders & proceedings of Sullivan Court thereon.
(p-129) But that the complainant shall nevertheless have leave to hold
up those parts of the bill for Supporting any Equitable Title as far as he
can support the same by other proof, than the defendants confession also
ordered to be continued and that commissions issue to plaintiff and Deft.

James Berry   )
  vs   ) Bill & Injunction
Thomas Amis   )

The death of the defendant suggested in abatement; Therefore it is ordered
by the Court that this cause be continued until next Term.

Andrew Greer Sen.)
    vs)   Bill & Injunction
Michael Montgomery)

For reasons appearing to the Court it is ordered that this cause be continued
and that commissions Issue for plaintiff and defendant.

Cotteral Bailey)
    vs)   Original Bill
Andrew Greer Sen.)

Rule of reference set aside and it is ordered by the court that publication
of testimony be made on the first Monday of August next: Commissions for
plaintiff and defendant.

(p-130)   David Wright)
           vs)   Original Bill
      Alexander Bain)

Ordered that this cause be continued.

Richard /Woods)
    vs)   Bill & Injunction
Batt Wood, Thomas Wood &)
Benjamin Gest)

For reasons appearing to the Court it is ordered that the judgment pro confesso
against Batt Wood be set aside & that his answer be received and filed also
that commissions issue for plaintiff and defendants.

Ruth Brown)
    vs)   Bill & Injunction
John McDowell)

Ordered by the Court to be continued.

William Cobb)
    vs)   Original Bill
William Conway & Others)

On motion of Counsel for the defendant it is ordered that time be given them
untill next Term to file their answers.

(p-131)   Michael Harrison)
           vs)   Bill & Injunction
      William Murphey &)
      Isaac Thomas)

Ordered that this cause be continued, and that commissions issue to the complainant.

Stockley Donalson)
    vs)   Bill and Injunction
John Shields)

Ordered by the Court to be continued.

William Evans   )
    vs   )   Original Bill
Nathaniel Davis and)
James Charters   )

On reading Bill and answer and on argument of Counsel for the plaintiff and
defendant, it is ordered adjudged and decreed by the Court here, It is
ordered that the demurrer be sustained and that the Bill of the complainant
be dismissed.

Samuel May Senr.   )
    vs   )   Original Bill
George Ingle, Henry Oldham)
& Nancy Oldham   )

(p-132)   On argument of Counsel for the plaintiff and defendants it is
ordered by the Court that this cause be continued & that publication be
made in the Knoxville Gazette in three successive numbers that Henry Oldham
do file his answer at the next Term, otherwise the Bill of the complainant
will be taken pro confesso and that a commission issue to take his answer
before the presiding judge of the County Court of -------

Edward Erwine   )
    vs   )   Original Bill
Benjamin Erwine   )

On motion of the plaintiff's attorney it is ordered that this cause be
continued and that commissions issue to plaintiff & defendant.

John Sharp   )
    vs   )   Original Bill
John Adair   )

It is ordered by the Court that this cause be continued and that commissions
issue to plaintiff and defendant.

(p-133)   John Blevins)
             vs   )   Original Bill
          John Shelby)

On Reading Bill and Answer and on argument of Counsel for plaintiff and defendant it is ordered adjudged and Decreed by the Court here that the complainants Injunction be dissolved and that his bill be retained as an
original.

John Laughlin &   )
Robert Craig   )
    vs   )   Original Bill
John Vance   )

It appearing to the Satisfaction of the Court that the defendant hath failed
to put in his answer agreeable to a rule made at March Term 1797 It is therefore ordered by the Court here that the Bill of the complainant be taken
pro confesso.

John Johnston   )
         vs   )   Bill & Injunction
Moses Carrick   )

It is ordered that this cause be continued untill next Term.

(p-134)   Thomas King   )
            vs   )   Original Bill
          Benoni Caldwel)
       Joel Gillenwater &)
       John Hall   )

For reasons appearing to the Court it is ordered by the Court that this cause
be continued and that commissions issue to plaintiff and defendant.

William Christmas   )
         vs   )   Original Bill
Nathaniel and Samuel Henderson   )

Ordered by the Court to be continued & that the defendants have time untill
next term to file their answer.

Michael Montgomery   )
         vs   )   Bill & Injunction
William Burk   )

Ordered by the Court to be continued & that the defendant have untill next
Term to file his answer.

Agnes Torbett   )
         vs   )   Original Bill
Alexander Torbett   )

Ordered by the Court to be continued and that commissions issue to plaintiff
and defendant.

(p-135)   Samuel Vance)
            vs   )   Bill and Injunction
          John Beard   )

Dismissed by written agreement.

John Millikin   )
         vs   )   Bill & Injunction
John Smith   )

Ordered by the Court that this cause be continued and that the defendant have
untill next Term to file his answer.

Andrew Greer   )   Sci fa made known in
      vs   )   presence of M. Rhea and
James Gains Bail for   )   Geo. Vincent.
Martin Armstrong   )   T. Shelby Snf.
Being solemnly called and having failed to appear, it is ordered by the Court
that judgment go against said Jas Gains according to Scire facias.

SEPTEMBER TERM 1798

(p-136) At a Court of Equity begun and held for the District of Washington in the town of Jonesborough, on the 17th Day of September in the year 1798.

Present the Honorable
Archibald Roane &) esqrs.
David Campbell)

Henderson & Company)
    vs   )   Original Bill
Henderson & Company)

It is ordered by the Court that this cause be continued.

John Waddell   )
    vs   )   Bill & Injunction
Robert Paterson   )

It is ordered by the Court that this cause be continued, and that the issues of fact made up in this cause be filed.

William Cocke   )
    vs   )   Original Bill
Richard Henderson & Co.)

For reasons appearing to the Court it is ordered this cause be continued (p-137) and that publication extend only to the Knoxville Gazette.

Austin Shoat   )
    vs   )   Bill and Injunction
Ephraim Dunlop   )

It is ordered by the Court that this cause be continued untill next Term.

William Gardener   )
    vs   )   Original Bill
Mary Looney & the heirs)
of Benjamin Looney decd.)

Ordered by the Court that this cause be continued untill next Term & that the issues of fact made up be filed.

John Carney   )
    vs   )   Original Bill
Ephraim Dunlop and the)
heirs of Ann Moor decd.)

It is ordered by the Court that this cause be continued, and publication be made in the Knoxville Gazette that the heirs and legal representatives of Ann Moor appear (p-138) at the next term and file their answers otherwise the bill of the complainant will be taken pro confesso.

Robert Keer   )
    vs   )   Bill & Injunction
Alexander Meek   )

It is ordered by the Court that this cause be continued and that commissions issue to plaintiff and Defendant.

David Boothe)
   vs)   Rehearing
Benjamin Ford &)
Garret Fitzgerald)

It is ordered by the Court that this cause be continued and that commissions issue for plaintiff and Defendants.

Laurence Kettron)
   vs)   Original Bill
John Keywood)

This cause was dismissed by the complainants attorney.

(p-139)   James Berry)
          vs)   Bill and Injunction
        Thomas Amis)

This cause was referred by written agreement filed.

Andrew Greer)
   vs)   Bill and Injunction
Michael Montgomery)

This cause was dismissed by consent of plaintiff and Defendant, each pays his own costs and the said Michael Montgomery relinquishes his judgment obtained at common law which is complained of in the complainants Bill of complaint, and that the said Andrew Greer be entitled to receive back all sums of money which he has paid to any person, in pursuance of the said judgment at common law.

Cottral Bailey)
   vs)   Retained as an Original
Andrew Greer)

By consent of plaintiff and defendant it is ordered by the court that this cause be referred to Landon Carter, Nathaniel Taylor, John Carter & David McNabb and their award to be a rule of this Court.

(p-140)   David Wright)
          vs)   Original Bill
        Alexander Bain)

For reasons appearing to the Court it is ordered that this cause be continued and that a commission issue to James Tapscot and McChenahan of ----- County Virginia empowering them on either of them to take the Answer of the Defendant Alexander Bain and it appearing to the satisfaction of the Court that the complainant has deceased since the commencement of this suit and this administrators appearing at this Term in open Court were admitted to revive, and that commissions issue to complaintiff and defendant.

Richard Woods)
   vs)   Bill & Injunction
Bat Wood, Thomas Wood)
and Benjamin Gist)

For reasons appearing to the Court it is ordered that this cause be continued
and that a Dureas tecum issue to the clerk of Green County Court, to bring
up the depositions filed in his office in a caveat had and tried between
the parties in the said County Court of Greene, also publication of Testamony
at this day, and that the issues of fact made up between the parties be fild.

(p-141) Ruth Brown   )
              vs   )   Bill & Injunction
         John McDowell   )

For reasons appearing to the Court it is ordered that this cause be continued
and revived against William Whitson Executor of the said John McDowell deceased and that commissions issue to plaintiff and defendant.

William Cobb   )
         vs   )   Bill & Injunction
William Conway & others   )

For reasons appearing to the Court it is ordered that this cause be
continued, & time untill next Term for Jesse Evans one of the defendants
to file his answer, to the amended Bill of the complainant, and also that
a commission issue to John Adams senr, John Adams Junr or either of them of
Wythe County Virginia empowering them to take the answer of the said Jessee
Evans.

Micheal Harrison   )
         vs   )   Retained as
William Murphy &   )   an original
Isaac Thomas   )

By consent of the plaintiff's and defendants attorney, it is ordered by the
Court that this cause be continued.

(p-142) Stockely Donaldson)
              vs   )   Bill and Injunction
         John Shields   )

On reading Bill and Answer it is ordered adjudged and decreed by the Court
that the complainants Bill of Injunction be dissolved.

Samuel May Senior   )
         vs   )   Original Bill
George Ingle, Henry Oldham   )
and Nancy Oldham   )

For reasons appearing to the Court it is ordered that this cause be continued
and that unless Nancy Oldham answer by her guardian Joshua Cox her husband
at the next term the Bill of the complainant will be taken pro confesso as to
herself.

Edward Erwine   )
         vs   )   Original Bill
Benjamine Erwine   )

The death of the complainant Suggested, it is ordered by the Court here that

Secre facias issue to the legal representatives to revive.

John Sharp	)	Retained as an
vs	)	original
John Adair	)	

It is ordered by the Court that this cause be continued, and that commissions issue to plaintiff & Defendant.

(p-143) | John Blevins |) | Retained as an |
| vs |) | Original |
| John Shelby |) | |

By the Court it is ordered that this cause be continued and by consent of complainant and Defendants it is agreed that the issues of fact be made up and tried at next Term, and that commissions issue to plaintiff and defendant.

John Laughlin & Robert Craig	)	
vs	)	Original Bill
John Vance	)	

The complainants Bill of complaint being taken pro confesso at March Term 1798 and being finally Settled at this term by the parties, it is therefore ordered by the Court to be Dismissed.

John Johnson	)	
vs	)	Bill and Injunction
Moses Carrick	)	

Ordered by the Court that this cause be continued and that commissions issue to plaintiff and defendant.

(p-144) | Thomas King |) | |
vs	)	Original Bill
Benoni Caldwell	)	
Joel Gillingwater &	)	
John Hall	)	

Ordered by the Court to be continued and that commissions issue to plaintiff and Defendant.

William Christmas	)	
vs	)	Original Bill
Nathaniel and Samuel Henderson	)	

Ordered by the Court that this cause be continued and that Nathaniel Henderson be and is hereby appointed guardian for Samuel Henderson, and that they have untill next Term to fill their answer.

Michael Montgomery	)	
vs	)	Bill & Injunction
William Burke	)	

Ordered by the Court that the defendant have untill next Term to file his answer and it appearing to the satisfaction of the Court that the defendant is not an inhabitant of this government, it is therefore ordered that a commission

issued to John Hunt and   (p-145)   Joshua Stockton of Fleming County State
of Kentucky empowering them to take the answer of the said William Burke.

Agnes Torbett	)	
vs	)	Original Bill
Alexander Torbett	)	

John Millikin	)	
vs	)	Bill and Injunction
John Smith	)	

Robert Coile	)	
vs	)	Bill & Injunction
The heirs of William Ingram decd.)		

For reasons appearing to the Court it is ordered that the foregoing causes
be continued untill next Term and that commissions issue for plaintiff and
Defendants.

John Coulter	)	
vs	)	Bill & Injunction
Richard Mitchell &	)	
Thomas Houghton	)	

Ordered by the Court that a subpoena to answer and copy of Bill issue to
the defendants.

William Shillern	)	
vs	)	Bill and Injunction
Nicholas Hawkins	)	

Ordered by the Court to be continued and that commissions issue to plaintiff
& defendant.

William P. Chester	)	
vs	)	Bill and Injunction
David Stewart	)	

Ordered by the Court that an alias Subpoena issue to the sheriff of Knox
County.

John Yancy	)	
vs	)	Original Bill
James Reed	)	

Ordered by the Court that the Defendant have untill next Term to answer.

It is ordered by the Court that David Deaderick of Washington County,
John Williams of Sullivan County, Thomas Jackson of Hawkins County, and
Landon Carter of Carter County, be and are hereby appointed commissions of
affidavits for the counties aforesaid respectively.

(p-147)   Ordered by the Court that James Roddye of Jefferson County be and
is hereby appointed guardian for Louis Russell a minor son of George Russell
deceased for the purpose of bringing a suit in Equity.

MARCH TERM 1799

(p-148)   At a Court of Equity began and in the Town of Jonesborough for
the District of Washington in the State of Tennessee, on the 14th day of
March 1799.

Present the Honorable
Archibald Roane, David
Campbell and Andrew Jackson

Esquires Judges of said Court.

Henderson & Company   )
      vs   )   Original Bill
Henderson & Company   )

John Waddle   )
    vs   )   Bill and Injunction
Robert Patterson   )

    It is ordered by the Court the foregoing causes be continued untill
next Term.

William Cocke   )
    vs   )   Original Bill
Richard Henderson & Company)

For reasons appearing it is therefore ordered by the Court that this cause
be continued & that publication in the Knoxville Gazette be renewed.

Auston Shoat   )
   vs   )   Bill and Injunction
Ephraim Dunlop   )

On motion and reasons shewn it is ordered by the Court there this cause be
continued and set for tryal at next term, also publication of Testamony
four months hence.

(p-149)   William Gardner   )
          vs   )   Original Bill
       Mary Looney & the heirs of)
       Benjamin Looney deceased)

For reason appearing to the Court it is ordered that this be continued and
the issues of fact made up under directions of the Court be filed and commissions for plaintiff and defendant also publication of Testamony five days
previous to next term.

John Carney   )
   vs   )   Original Bill
Ephraim Dunlop & the)
Heirs of Ann Moore decd.)

For reasons appearing to the Court it is ordered that this cause be continued
untill next term and that commissions issue to plaintiff and defendant.

Robert Keer   -   compt.)
      vs   )   Bill & Injunction
Alexander Meek - Deft.)

For reasons appearing to the Court it is ordered that this cause be continued untill next term and commissions issue to the Defendant.

David Boothe   -   compt.)
      vs   )   Rehearing
Benjamin Ford &   ) Defts.)
Garret Fitzgarald)   )

On the 14th day of March 1799 the foregoing cause   (p-150)   came on to be tryed when also came a Jury (to wit) Jesse Pain, Christopher Taylor, Jacob Brown, Joseph Young, Isaac White, James Hay, Andrew Greer, Thomas Hughes, Timothy Acoff, Samuel Wilson, Michael Montgomery, & James Galbreath to well and truly try the following issues of fact (to wit) whether any and what were the conditions on which David Boothe put into the hands of Benjamin Ford a negroe girl named Bet whether a tender of the sum money Thirty four pounds five shillings Virginia money was made by David Boothe or any other person for him to Garret Fitzgerrald or Benjamin Ford, and if any at what time & what is the value of the Services of the negroe girl Bet by the year. On their oaths do find and say lst. we find the negro wench was put into the hands of Benjamin Ford for the payment of thirty four pounds five shillings Virginia money to be paid by David Boothe; 2nd. we find no Lawfull tender to be made by said Boothe or any other person for him; 3rd. we find the yearly Services of the said wench to be worth the interest of said thirty four pounds five shillings and paying taxes for said wench and finding her clothes and on arguments of Counsel Learned in the Law for complainants and defendant, it is   (p-151)   ordered adjudged and Decreed this Honorable Court that the Bill of the Complainant be Dismissed with Costs.

James Berry   compt.   )
      vs   )   Bill & Injunction
Thomas Amis   deft.   )

For reasons appearing it is ordered by the Court that this be continued untill next Term and that the rule of reference made at last Term be Set aside and that commissions issue for plaintiff and deft. twenty days notice to the adverse party for taking depositions publication of Testamony on the first day of the next Term.

Cottral Bailey   compt.)
      vs   )   Retained as an
Andrew Greer   Deft.   )   Original

For reasons appearing it is ordered by the Court that this cause be continued untill next term, and that the rule of reference made at the last term be set aside also commissions issue for plaintiff & defendant and that publication of Testamony five days previous to next term.

David Wright -   compt.)
      vs   )   Original Bill
Alexander Bain - Deft.)

For reasons appearing to the Court it is therefore ordered that this cause
be   (p-152)   continued and publication be inserted in the Knoxville Gazette that the defendant Alexr Baine file his answer on the first day of
the next Term otherwise the Bill of the complainant will taken pro confesso
it is also ordered by this Honorable Court that a commission issue to
James Tapscott and McClenahan of Bothecourt County and state of Virginia empowering them and each of them to take the answer of Alexander Baine.

```
Richard Woods   -  compt.  )
        vs                 )        Bill & Injunction
Batt Wood, Thomas  ) Defts.)
Wood & Benjamin Gest)      )
```

For reasons appearing it is ordered by the Court that this cause be continued untill next term a resurvey being prayed by the Defendants on the
premises in dispute which was granted accordingly and that Daniel Rawlings
be and is here by appointed surveyor to perform the same.

```
Ruth Brown  ⊖ compt.   )
     vs                )        Bill & Injunction
John McDowell - Deft.  )
```

For reasons appearing it is ordered by the Court that this cause be continued
and that commissions issue for plaintiff and deft. a written argument filed.

```
(p-153)    William Cobb - compt.       )
               vs                      )        Original Bill
           William Conway & others - Defts. )
```

For reasons appearing it is ordered by the Court that this cause be continued
untill next term and that commissions issue for plaintiff and defendant.

```
Michael Harrison   - compt.)
     vs                    )        Retained as an Original
William Murphy & ) Defts.  )
Isaac Thomas     )         )
```

For reasons appearing it is ordered by the Court that this cause be continued.

```
Samuel May Senr. - compt.        )
     vs                          )        Original Bill
George Ingle, Henry Oldham ) Defts.)
& Nancy Oldham             )     )
```

Nancy Oldham one of the defendants in this cause having failed to enter her
appearance agreeable to an order of publication made at Sept. 1798. It is
therefore ordered that the bill of the complainants be taken pro confesso
as her, and it appearing to the Satisfaction of the Court that Henry Oldham
an other deft. is not an inhabitant of this state, it is therefore ordered
that   (p-154)   publication be inserted in the Knoxville Gazette or Nashville in two Successive numbers that unless he appear at the next term and
file his answer the Bill of the complainant will be taken pro confesso as to
him and that commissions issue for plaintiff and deft.

```
Edward Erwine  - compt.)
        vs            )      Original Bill
Benjamin Erwine - Deft.)
```

Joseph McMinn Executor of the last will and Testament of Edward Erwine deceased, by his attorney comes into court and revives this suit, it is therefore ordered by the court to be continued untill next Term.

```
John Sharp  - comp. )
        vs          )    Retained as
John Adair  - Deft. )    an original
```

For reasons appearing it is ordered by the court that this cause be continued untill next Term.

```
John Blevins  - compt.)
        vs            )    Retained as
John Shelby   - Deft. )    an original
```

This cause continued untill next Term by written agreement filed it is therefore ordered by the court that coms. issue for plaintiff & deft.

```
(p-155)   John Johnston - compt.)
              vs            )      Bill & Injunction
          Moses Carrick - Deft. )
```

```
Thomas King  - compt.      )
        vs                 )      Original Bill
Bononi Caldwell - )        )
Joel Gillenwater &) - Defts.)
John Hall        )         )
```

For reasons appearing it is ordered by the court that the foregoing causes be continued untill next Term.

```
William Christmas - Compt.      )
        vs                      )      Original Bill
Nathl & Samuel Henderson - Defts.)
```

The defendants having failed to Enter their appearance agreeable to a rule heretofore made by this Honorable Court it is therefore ordered that the bill of the complainant be taken proconfesso. On motion of the Defendants attorney it is ordered by the court that the Rule pro confesso be set aside and answer filed. On motion it is ordered by the court they have leave untill next Term to amend their answer.

```
Michael Montgomery - Compt.)
        vs                 )      Bill & Injunction
William Burk       - Deft. )
```

On the 15th day of March 1799 this cause   (p-156)   came on to be tryed Bill and Answer being read, it is ordered by the Court that the Injunction of the complainant be Dissolved and on motion the bill retained as an original and leave to amend the same.

Agnes Torbott - Compt.   )
      vs   )   Original Bill
Alexander Torbett - Deft.)

    For reasons appearing it is ordered by the Court that this cause be
continued untill next Term, and that commissions issue to complainant and
defendant, publication of Testamony on the first day of the next Term.

John Mileken - Compt.)
     vs   )   Bill and Injunction
John Smith   - Deft.)

Robert Kile - Compt.   )
    vs   )   To perpetuate
the Heirs of William) Defts.)   Testamony
Ingram deceased   )   )

    For reasons appearing it is ordered by the Court the foregoing Causes
be continued untill next Term and that commission issue to plaintiffs and
defts.

(p-157)   John Coulter - Compt.   )
              vs   )   Bill & Injunction
          Richard Mitchell &) Defts.)
          Thomas Houghton   )   )

    Ordered by the Court that this cause be continued untill the next
term for the answer of Thomas Houghton.

William Skillern - Compt.)
     vs   )   Bill & Injunction
Nicholas Hawkins - Deft.)

    For reasons appearing it is ordered by the Court that this cause be
continued untill next Term and that commissions issue to plaintiff and deft.
Publication of Testamony on the first day of the next Term.

William P. Chester - Comptl.)
    vs   )   Bill & Injunction
David Stuart   - Deft.)

    This cause Dismissed for _verball_ order of the complainant the Defendant
assumes the costs.

(p-158)   John Yancy - Compt.)
             vs   )   Original Bill
          James Reed - Deft.)

    For reasons appearing it is ordered by the Court that this cause be
continued untill next Term and that the Deft. have leave untill next Term
to amend his Answer.

Mark Mitchell - Compt.)
     vs   )   Bill & Injunction
Michael Montgomery -Deft.)

On reading bill and answer and arguments of counsel for plaintiff and deft. the court ordered this cause to be continued untill next term and that commissions issue to plaintiff and deft. Publication of Testamony the first Saturday of next Term.

James King - Compt.)
    vs   )   Bill & Injunction
John Overton &) Defts.)
David Allison)   )

On reading bill and answer and on arguments of counsel for plaintiff and Defendant it is ordered by the Court (p-159) that the injunction of the complainant be Dissolved and that the Defendant have the benefit of his Judgment at Law.

John Sevier Jun. - compt.)
    vs   )   Bill & Injunction
Samuel Jackson)   )
John B. Evans &) Defts.)
David Allison)   )

For reasons appearing it is ordered by the Court that this cause be continued untill the next Term, and that a commission issue to the mayor of the corporation of George Town, State of Maryland to take the answer of Saml Jackson one of the Defendants also one other commission to the mayor of City of Philadelphia to take the answer of John B. Evans, the Deft.

Lawrence Horn - Compt.)
    vs   )   Bill & Injunction
Thomas Gibbons - Deft.)

For reasons appearing it is ordered by the Court that this cause be continued and that the Defendant have untill next Term to file his answer.

(p-160)   William Russell & others - Compts.)
            vs   )   Bill & Injunction
         The Heirs of Richard &   )   )
         William Caswell,Deceased &) Defts.)
         against Joseph Blair   )   )

For reason appearing it is ordered by the Court that this cause be continued and the Defendants have untill next Term to answer.

Benjamin Cutbirth - Compt.)
    vs   )   Bill & Injunction
Elizabeth Dotson &) Defts.)
Nathl Taylor, Admr.)   )

On reading bill and answer and on argument of counsel for plaintiff and Defendant it is ordered by the Court that the injunction of the complainant be Dissolved and on motion it was also ordered the bill be retained as an original.

On the 27th of April 1799 the above cause Dismissed per written order of the compt.

Thomas King & others - Compts.)
        vs   )   Bill & Injunction
James Daniel   - Deft.)

On reading bill and answer and argument of Counsel for complainants and (p-161) defendant it is ordered by the Court that the complainants injunction be Dissolved. On motion the bill retained as an original.

SEPTEMBER TERM 1799

At a Court of Equity begun and held in the Town of Jonesborough for the District of Washington in the State of Tennessee, on the 12th day of September 1799.

Present the Honorable
Archibald Roane   )
David Campbell &) Esquires
Andrew Jackson   )

Henderson & Co.)
     vs   )   Original Bill
Henderson & Co.)

For reasons appearing it is ordered by the Court that this cause be continued untill next Term.

John Waddle - Compt.   )
    vs   )   Bill & Injunction
Robert Patterson - Deft.)

Ordered by the Court that this cause be contd.

(p-162)   William Cocke - Compt.   )
               vs   )   Original Bill
       Richard Henderson & Co. - Defts.)

This cause Dismissed per verball order of the complainant.

Auston Shoat - Compt.)
    vs   )   Bill & Injunction
Ephraim Dunlop - Deft.)

On the 13th of September 1799 this cause came to be heard, bill and answer being read, it is ordered adjudged and Decreed by the Court that the injunction of the complainant be Dissolved and bill Dismissed.

William Gardner - Compt.   )   Original Bill
    vs   )
Mary Looney & the Heirs of) Defts.)
Benjamin Looney, Deceased)   )

On the 12th day of September 1799 the foregoing cause came to be Tried, whereupon came a Jury (to wit) Benjamin Holland, Daniel Hamlen, John Bayless, Joseph Crouch, Thomas Prater, David Russell (p-163)   John Wear, John

Newman,.Richard Mitchell, Isaac Tipton, Samuel Wood & Robert Alison, who being impanneled and sworn to well and truly try the following issues of Fact (to wit) whether a contract took place between the said Benjamin Looney in his life time and the said William Gardner concerning said Land as stated in the complainants Bill and if a contract did take place what it was.

2d. Whether said William Gardner has paid the purchase money stipulated to be paid by him for said Land, and if the whole has not been paid, what part; and if all or any part has been paid; in what manner, at what time and to whom, has the same been paid.

3d. If any contract was made between the said Benjamin in his lifetime and the said William as Stated in the complainants Bill, whether the same has been revoked by the said Benjamin and William on their oaths do say 1st, we find that a contract did take place between the complainant William Gardner & Benjamin Loony as stated in the bill of complaint. 2nd. we find that the purchase money was paid by Gardner to Benjamin Loony. 3rd. we find that no (p-164) revocation ever was made between the parties.

For reasons appearing it is ordered by the Court that this cause be continued untill next Term for a final Decree.

John Carney – compt.   )
            vs   )   Original Bill
Ephraim Dunlop &   ) Defts.)
Heirs of Ann Moore, Decd.)   )

The Heirs of Ann Moore Deceased having failed to enter their appearance agreeable to an order of publication made at September Term 1798, it is therefore ordered by the Court that the Bill of Complainant be Taken pro confesso as to them.

Robert Keer – compt.   )
            vs   )   Bill & Injunction
Alexander Meek – Deft.)

For reasons appearing it is ordered by the Court that this cause be continued untill next Term and that commissions issue to complainant and defendant.

James Berry – Compt.)
            vs   )   Bill & Injunction
Lucy Amis – Deft.   ).

For reasons appearing it is ordered by the Court that this cause be continued untill next   (p-165)   Term and that commissions issue to plaintiff and defendant publication of Testimony.

Cottral Bailey – Compt.)
            vs   )   Retained as
Andrew Greer   – Deft.)   an original

On the 14th day of September 1799 this cause came on to be tried, bill and answer being read, the defendant having demurred to part of the complainants Bill and on motion that the demurrer be sustained the Court took an advisare as to the demurer issue of fact on the plea to be tried at the next Term commissions to both parties, publication of Testimony five months hence.

```
David Wright - compt.    )
        vs               )        Original Bill
Alexander Baine - Deft.  )
```

For reasons appearing it is ordered by the Court that this cause be continued untill next Term commissions issue to compt. and defendant thirty days notice to be given for taking depositions in the State of Virginia.

```
Richard Woods - compt.              )
        vs                          )    Bill & Injunction
Batt Wood, Thomas Wood & ) Defts.)  )
Benjamin Gist            )          )
```

(p-166)   A Survey of the premisses in dispute being prayed for by the Defendants attorney it is ordered by Court that it be granted and that Daniel Rawlings on the part of the defendants and James Galbreath on the part of complainant be and are hereby appointed and empowered to perform same and make return to the next Term and commissions issue compt. and defendants.

```
Ruth Brown - compt.    )
     vs                )    Bill & Injunction
John McDowell - Deft.  )
```

For reasons appearing it is ordered by the Court that this Cause be continued untill the next Term, publication of Testimony five months hence and forty days notice to the adverse party for taking depositions in the State of North Carolina.

```
William Cobb - complainant       )
        vs                       )    Original Bill
William Conway & others- Defts.) )
```

For reasons appearing it is ordered by the Court that this cause be continued & commissions issue to compt. and defts. thirty days notice for taking depositions in the State of Virginia, publication of Testimony five months hence.

```
(p-167)   Michael Harrisson - compt.)
             vs                      )    Retained as
          William Murphy & ) Defts.  )    an original
          Isaac Thomas    )    )
```

For reasons appearing it is ordered by the Court that this cause be continued untill the next Term.

```
Samuel May Senr- compt.              )
        vs                           )    Original Bill
George Ingle, Henry Oldham & ) Defts.)
Nancy Oldham                 )   )
```

Henry Oldham one of the Defendants in this cause not having entered his appearance agreeable to an order of publication made at March Term 1799, it is therefore ordered by the Court that the bill of the complainant be taken proĉonfesso as to him publication of Testimony five months hence.

Joseph McMinn - Exer of)- Compt.)
Edward Erwine decd.   )   )   Original Bill
      vs   )
Benjamine Erwine - Deft.   )

On the 13th day of September 1799 this cause came to be heard bill and
answer being read   (p-168)   in presence of Counsel for complainant and
defendant the court say they will advise of this cause untill next Term.

John Sharp - compt.)
    vs   )   Retained as
John Adair - Deft.)   an original

For reasons appearing it is ordered by the Court that this cause be
continued, untill next Term, and commissions issue to plaintiff and Defendant
publication of Testimony on the first day of February next issues of fact
made up under the directions of the Court and ordered to be filed.

John Blevins - compt.)
    vs   )   Retained as
John Shelby - Deft.)   an original

For reasons appearing it is ordered by the Court that this cause be continued untill the next Term and commissions issue to complainant and Defendant
Publication of Testimony Six months hence, issues of fact made up under the
directions of the Court and ordered to be filed.

(p-169)   John Johnston - compt.)
             vs   )   Bill & Injunction
         Moses Carrick- deft.)

For reasons appearing it is ordered by the Court that this Cause be
continued untill the next Term and commissions issue to complainant and defendants. Publication of Testimony five months hence.

Thomas King - compt.   )
      vs   )   Original Bill
Benoni Caldwell   )   )
Joel Gillenwater &   ) Defts.)
John Hall   )   )

For reasons appearing it is ordered by the Court this cause be continued
untill the next Term, and commissions issue to plaintiff and Defendant.

William Christmas - Compt.   )
      vs   )   Original Bill
Nathl & Saml Henderson - Defts.)

For reasons appearing it is ordered by the Court that the Defendants
have leave untill next Term to amend their answers.

Michael Montgomery - compt.)
      vs   )   Retained as an original
William Burke   - Deft.)

It is ordered by the Court that this cause be contd untill the next Term.

(p-170)   Agness Torbett - compt.   )
               vs   )   Original Bill
           Alexander Torbett - Deft.)

On motion for a rule of reference which was not admitted ordered by the Court that this cause be continued untill next Term and that commissions issue to compt. and defendant publication of Testimony five months hence.

John Miliken - compt.)
       vs   )   Bill & Injunction
John Smith - Deft.)

For reasons appearing it is ordered by the Court that this Cause be continued untill the next Term, and that commissions issue to the complainant.

Robert Kile - compt.   )
      vs   ) To perpetuate Testamony
Richard Mitchell &) Defts.)
Thomas Ingram   )   )

Ordered by the Court that this cause be continued untill next Term, and that commissions issue to the complainant.

John Coulter - compt.   )
      vs   )   Bill & Injunction
Richard Mitchell &) Defts.)
Thomas Houghton   )   )

For reasons appearing it is ordered by the Court that this cause be continued   (p-171)   untill the next Term, and that a commission issue to Judge Walton of the State of Georgia empowering him to receive upon oath the answer of Thomas Houghton, and in the mean time a publication be inserted in two Successive numbers of the Knoxville Gazette that unless Thomas Houghton one of the Defendants enter his appearance at the next term the bill of the complainant will be taken pro confesso as to him, and that a Survey of the premises in dispute be made and Joseph Cobb is hereby appointed & empower to perform the same.

William Skillern - compt.)
      vs   )   Bill & Injunction
Nicholas Hawkins - Deft.)

For reasons appearing it is ordered by the Court that this cause be continued untill next Term and commissions issue to compt. & deft. thirty days notice to the adverse party for taking depositions in the State of Kentucky also twenty days in Washington County State of Virginia. Publication of Testamony five months hence.

(p-172)   John Yancy - compt.)
             vs   )   Original Bill
           James Reed - Deft.)

For reasons appearing it is ordered by the Court that this cause be continued untill the next Term and commissions issue to complainant and defendant publication of Testimony on the first day of next Term.

Mark Mitchell - compt.   )
    vs   )   Bill & Injunction
Michael Montgomery - Deft.)

For reasons appearing it is ordered by the Court that this cause be continued untill the next Term and commissions issue to the complainant.

John Sevier Jun. - compt.)
    vs   )   Bill & Injunction
Saml Jackson   )   )
John B. Evans &) - Defts.)
David Allison   )   )

This cause dismissed per Verball order of the complainant September the 3d 1799.

(p-173) Lawrence Horn - compt.)
        vs   )   Bill & Injunction
    Thomas Gibbons - Deft.)

For reasons appearing it is ordered by the Court that this cause be continued, and that the defendant have time untill the fourth day of the next Term to answer.

William Russell & others - compts.   )
    vs   )   Bill & Injunction
The Heirs of William & Richard)   )
Caswell deceased & against   ) Defts.)
Joseph Blair   )   )

Ordered by the Court that this cause be continued and Joseph Blair one of the Defendants have leave untill the first day of the next Term to file his answer otherwise the bill of the complainants will be taken pro confesso and that publication be inserted in the Knoxville Gazette that the other defendant appear on the first day of the next and file their answers otherwise the bill of complainants will be taken pro confesso to them.

Thomas King & others - compts.)
    vs   )   Retained as an
James Daniel   - Deft.)   original

For reasons appearing it is ordered by the Court that this cause be Dismissed with costs.

(p-174) James Reed - compt.)
        vs   )   Original Bill
    John Adams &) Defts.)
    Jacob Sooman)   )

For reasons appearing it is ordered by the Court that this cause be continued untill the next Term.

Robert Allen - compt.   )
      vs   ) Bill & Injunction
Archibald Blackburn - Deft.)

    The defendant having failed to enter his appearance agreeable to the
rules of this Court it is therefore order by the Court that the bill of complainant be taken pro confesso.

John Pitner - compt.   )
      vs   ) Bill & Injunction
Robert & Thomas Rogers - Deft.)

    Bill and answer being read and on arguments of counsel for complainant
and defendant it is ordered by the Court that the Injunction of the complainant
be Dissolved, and on motion of the complainants attorney it is ordered by
the Court that the bill be retained as an original and the Defendnat Robert
Rogers have the benefit of his Judgment at Law on his giving bond with Sufficient Security to pay back the money should the complainant hereafter recover on his said bill, commissions for complainant and defendant.

(p-175)   Robert Alison - compt.   )
          vs   ) Original Bill
      Isaac Shelby   )   )
      William Hughes &) Defts.)
      Elizabeth Hughes)   )

    For reasons appearing it is ordered by the Court that this cause be
continued untill the next Term and that alias subpoena issue against William
& Elizabeth Hughes the other Defendants.

Thomas King - compt.)
      vs   ) Bill & Injunction
John Smith - Deft.)

    For reasons appearing it is order by the Court that this cause be continued
untill next Term, and alias Subpoena issue against the Defendant to Hawkins
County.

Alexander Nelson - compt.)
      vs   ) Bill & Injunction
Philip North -   Deft.)

    For reasons appearing it is ordered by the Court that this cause be in-
serted in the Knoxville and Winchester Gazettes, that the defendant appear
here on the first day of the next Term and file his answer otherwise the
bill of the complainant will be taken pro confesso (p-176) ordered by
the court that the following notices shall be given to the adverse parties
of the time and place of taking Testimony on all commissions here after issued
unless where it may be otherwise specially directed. In the State of Tennessee twenty days In state of Kentucky Thirty days in the State of Virginia,
Forty days in the State of North Carolina Forty days in the State of South
Carolina Forty days in State of Maryland Forty five days in the State of
Pennsylvania Fifty days

MARCH TERM 1800

At a Court of Equity begun and held in the State of Tennessee for the District of Washington in the Town of Jonesborough on the 13th day of March 1800.

Present the Honorable
Archibald Roane) Esquires
David Campbell) Judges of said
Andrew Jackson) Court

(p-177) Henderson & Company - compts.)
vs)
Henderson & Company - Defts.)

On the 14th of March 1800 this cause came to be heard on motion the Court order that a Decree be made in conformity with a Deed of Partition made and Executed by John William, James Hogg, Richard Bullock, Walter Alves, Joseph Hart, John Umstead, Thomas Hart by his attorney Nathaniel Hart & Leonard Henderson original proprietors on the Eighth day of August one thousand Seven hundred and ninety seven.

John Waddle - compt.   )
vs) Bill & Injunction
Robert Patterson - Deft.)

Ordered by the Court that this cause be continued, the complainants death suggested then ordered by the Court to be Dismissed agreeable to a written agreement filed Robt & Thomas King, assumes costs.

William Gardner - compt.   )
vs) Original Bill
Mary Loony &Heirs of) Defts.)
Benjamin Loony deceased.)   )

For reasons appearing it is ordered by the Court this cause be continued untill next Term for a final Decree.

(p-178) John Carney - compt.   )
vs) Original Bill
Ephraim Dunlop &) Defts.)
Heirs of Ann Moore Decd.)   )

For reasons appearing it is ordered by the Court that this cause be continued and publication of Testimony on the first day of the next Term; issues of fact made up and filed under directions of the Court, also that commissions did po issue to compt. and defendants.

Robert Keer - compt.)
vs) Bill and Injunction
Alexr Meek - Deft.)

For reasons appearing it is ordered by the Court that this cause be continued untill the next Term and that commissions did po issue to the defendant.

James Berry   - Complt.   )
     vs   )   Injunction
Lucy Amis Executrix of) Deft.)
Thomas Amis Deceased   )   )

     For reasons appearing it is ordered by the court that this cause be
continued untill the next term , issues of fact made up and filed by consent
of the parties.

(p-179)   Cottral Bailey - compt.)
          vs   )   Retained as an original
      Andrew Greer   - Deft.)

For reasons appearing it is ordered by the court that this cause be continued
and that commission issue to complainant and defendant issues of fact filed
under the directions of the Court. Publication of Testimony on the first day
of the next term.

David Wright - compt.)
    vs   )   Original Bill
Alexr Baine   - Deft)

Ordered by the Court that this cause be continued untill the next term, and
that commissions did po issue to compt. and defendant,publication.of Testimony on the first day of the next term.

Richard Woods - compt.   )
    vs   )   Bill and Injunction
Batt Wood, Thomas Wood &)   Defts.)
Benjamin Gist   )   )

Ordered by the court that this cause be continued untill the next term, and
commissions issue to compt. and Defendnats.

(p-180)   Ruth Brown - compt.   )
         vs   )   Bill and Injunction
      William Whitson Exr.) Deft.)
      Of John McDowell decd.)   )

For reasons appearing it is ordered by the court that this cause be continued
untill the next Term. Issues made up and filed by consent of the parties.

William Cobb - compt.   .   )
    vs   )   Original Bill
William Conway & others - defts.)

Ordered by the court this cause be continued untill the next Term, and that
commissions issue to compt. and defendant.

Michael Harrison - compt.   )
    vs   )   Retained as an original
William Murphy and)   Defts.)
Isaac Thomas   )   )

     Ordered by the court that this cause be continued untill the next Term.

```
Samuel May  - compt.         )
        vs                   )        Original Bill
George Engle, Henry Oldham.& ) )
Nancy Oldham                 ) )
```

On the 14th of March this cause came to be   (p-181)   heard, whereupon it
appearing to the court that the bill of complainant, was taken pro confesso
as against Henry Oldham and Nancy Oldham defendants to the said bill, and
that George Engle one of the defendants to the said bill, has disclaimed all
right Ritle and interest to the Land mentioned in the said bill of complaint
and has confessed in his answer to the said bill that he has conveyed the right
Title and interest to the said Nancy Oldham. It is therefore ordered by the
court that the said Nancy Oldham and Joshua Cox her guardian and Husband, convey to the said complainant Samuel May Senr. all the legal and Equitable
right Title and interest, that were vested in the said Nancy Oldham by the
conveyance made to her by the said George Engle or in and to the said tract
of land mentioned in the said bill of complaint; and that the said complainant
Samuel May Senr. recover his costs against the said defendants Henry Oldham
and Nancy Oldham; and that the said George Engle be hence dismissed without
costs.

```
Joseph McMinn, Exr. of   )
Edward Erwine Decd.      )       Original Bill
        vs               )
Benjamin Erwine, Deft    )
```

On the 14th of March this cause came on to be heard, Bill and answer being
read, and   (p-182)   Several exhibits, and on the Argument of Counsel for
complainant and defendant.

The Court do order that a Decree be made up that the Bond mentioned in the
Complainants bill, Executed by Edward deceased, to Benjamin Erwin be delivered
up to be cancelled, and that the defendant pay the costs of this suit.

```
John Sharp - compt.)
      vs           )        Retained as an original
John Adair - Deft. )
```

On the 13th of March this cause came to be heard when also came a Jury, (to
wit) Isaac White, James Hays, John Weir, John Gass, James Penny, David Russell
of Washington, Timothy Acoff, Andrew Greer, John Criner, Robert Allison, Joseph
Crocket & David Russell of Greene, who being impanneled and sworn , well and
truly to try the following issues of fact (to wit) whether the complainant
and defendant revoked their contract concerning said Land, as stated in the
answer of the defendant, and whether a Tender of the balance remaining due on
the Bond, given by the complainant, and if made, at what time, said Tender was
made. On their oath do find that the contract was revoked as mentioned in
the defendants answer, and the complainant did not Tender the money as stated
in his bill of complaint. On which the complainant moved for a rule to show
cause why a new trial should be granted; ordered by the Court that the Rule
for a   (p-183)   new trial be discharged.

```
John Blevins - compt.)
      vs             )        Retained as an original
John Shelby  - Deft. )
```

On the 13th of March this cause came to be heard, when also came a Jury (to wit) Isaac White, James Hays, John Weir, John Gass, James Penny, David Russell of Greene County, William Anderson, Timothy Acoff, John Criner, John Fegan, Joseph Crocket, and David Russell of Washington County, who being impanneled and sworn, well and truly to try the following issues of fact, (to wit) whether the complainant lived on the land mentioned in his bill by the permission and consent of the respondent, and if so, whether any argument was made between the parties, that he the complainant was not to pay any thing for the use and occupation of the same, untill the final deter- mination of a suit between the respondent and William Blevins , concerning a tract of land of the said Land was a part and if the above agreement was entered into, at what time.

On their oath do find that the complainant lived on the land mentioned in his bill by permission of the respondents. We also (p-184) find that there was an agreement between the parties that the complainant was to live on the land without paying rent, untill the suit in Equity William Blevins and others against the said Shelby was determined -- We further find the agreement took place in the spring of the year 1793 -- whereupon the Court order the cause to be continued untill next Term for a final hearing.

```
John Johnston  -  compt.)
       vs              )      Bill and injunction
Moses Carrick  -  Deft. )
```

Ordered by the Court that this cause be contigued on the same Rule of last Term —

```
Thomas King  - Compt.            )
       vs                        )      Original Bill
Benoni Caldwell, Joel  ) Defts.)
Gillenwater & John Hall)         )
```

Ordered by the Court that this Cause be continued untill next Term. Publication of Testimony at the end of five months.

```
William Christmas  - compt.  )
       vs                    )      Original Bill
Nathl & Saml Henderson - Defts.)
```

For reasons appearing it is ordered by the Court (p-185) Court that this be continued untill the next Term, and that commissions did po issue to the complainant and defendant, forty days notice to the adverse party for taking depositions in the State of North Carolina.

```
Michael Montgomery - compt.)
       vs                  )      retained as an
William Burke  -  Deft.    )        original
```

For reasons appearing it is ordered by the Court that this Cause be continued untill the next term.

```
Agness Torbett  - compt.)
       vs               )      Original Bill
Alexr Torbett  -  Deft. )
```

On the 14th of March this cause came to be heard, and on reading bill and

answer, and the several depositions on both sides, the Court ordered the
complainants Bill of Complaint to be Dismissed with Costs.

```
John Meliken  -  compt.)
        vs            )   Bill and Injunction
John Smith    -  Deft. )
```

For reasons appearing it is ordered by the Court (p-186) that this cause
be continued untill the next term, and that commissions did po issue to the
complainant publication of Testimony five months hence.

```
Robert Kile  - compt.        )
        vs                   )   To perpetuate Testimony
The Heirs of William ) Defts.)
Ingram Deceased -    )       )
```

Ordered by the Court that cause be continued untill the next Term, and that
commissions issue to complainant.

```
John Coulter  - compt.      )
        vs                  )   Bill and Injunction
Richard Mitchell & ) Defts. )
Thomas Houghton    )
```

On motion it is ordered by the Court that a publication be inserted in the
Knoxville Gazette that Thomas Houghton one of the defendants in this cause,
appear on the first day of the next Term, and file his answer otherwise the
bill of the complainant will be taken proconfesso. Also that a commission
issue to Judge Walton of the State of Georgia impowering him to take the
answer of the said Thos. Houghton.

```
(p-187)   William Skillern  - compt.)
              vs                    )   Bill and Injunction
          Nicholas Hawkins  - Deft. )
```

Ordered by the Court that this cause be continued, and that publication of
Testimony be inlarged to the first day of next Term also commissions did po
issue to complainant and defendant, and thirty days Notice be given to the
adverse party for taking depositions in the state of Kentucky Forty days in
the State of Virginia.

```
John Yancy  -  compt.)
        vs           )   Original Bill
James Reed  -  Deft. )
```

Ordered by the Court that this Cause be continued untill the next Term.
Publication of Testimony inlarged to first day of the next term, and that
commissions did po issue to complainant and defendant thirty days notice to
the adverse party for taking depositions in the State of Kentucky and Forty
days in the State of Virginia.

```
Mark Mitchell  - compt.  )
        vs               )   Bill and Injunction
Michael Montgomery - Deft.)
```

(p-188)   Ordered by the Court that this cause be continued untill the next term, and that commissions did po issue to the complainant.

```
Lawrence Horn  -  compt.)
        vs             )   Bill and Injunction
Thomas Gibbons - Deft. )
```

On the 14th day of March this cause came to be heard, bill and answer being
read the Defendants Counsel moved that the Injunction of the complainant be
Dissolved, on argument the motion was over ruled by the Court, and ordered to
be held up till a final hearing; and that commissions issue to complainant
and defendant.

```
William Russell & others  - compt.      )
            vs                          )   Bill & Injunction
The Heirs of William & Richard )        )
Caswell deceased & against     )  Defts.)
Joseph Blair                   )        )
```

On motion of the defendants counsel it is ordered by the Court that the Rule
pro confesso made at September term 1799 be set aside. Plea in abatement filed
and Sustained, and the complainants Bill dismissed as to Joseph Blair. On
motion of the complainants counsel that the last order in this Cause be re-
considered whereupon the Court order that the plea in (p-189) abatement
be Set aside, and that Joseph Blair have leave untill the next term to plead
answer or demur, and that the Bill of the complainants be taken pro confesso
as to the Heirs of William & Richard Caswell deceased.

```
James Reed  - Compt. )
        vs           )   Original Bill
John Adams & ) Defts.)
Jacob Sooman )       )
```

On the 15th of March this cause came to be heard, on reading the complainants Bill and the Defendants having demur'd thereto. It is ordered by
the Court that the demurer be Set aside and time untill next term for the defendants to answer.

```
Robert Allen  - compt.  )
        vs              )   Bill and Injunction
Archibald Blackborn - Deft. )
```

For reasons appearing to the Court it is ordered that the rule entered at the
last Term be set aside, and the answer of the respondant be filed, and commissions did po issue to complainant and defendant, Publication of Testimony
on the first day of the next Term.

```
(p-190)   John Pitner - compt.      )
            vs                      ) Retained as an original
          Robert & Thomas Rogers - Defts.)
```

Ordered by the Court that this Cause be continued untill the next Term, and
commissions did po issue to the complainant and defendant, Thirty days
notice to the adverse party for taking Testimony in the State of Kentucky.

Robert Allison - compt.   )
    vs   )   Original Bill
Isaac Shelby & others - Defts.)

For reasons appearing it is ordered by the Court that this cause be continued
untill the next Term, and it appearing that Elizabeth Hughes one of the Defendants having failed to enter her appearance it is also ordered that alias
Subpoena and copy of the bill issue against the said Elizabeth to answer at
the next Term.

Thomas King - compt.)
    vs   )   Bill and Injunction
John Smith - Deft.)

The defendant having failed to enter his appearance agreeable to the rules of
this Court it is therefore ordered by the Court, that a publication be inserted in the Knoxville Gazette that the said Defendant John Smith   (p-191)
enter his appearance at the next Term otherwise the bill of the complainant
will be taken pro confesso and that a commission issue to John Wilson and
George Adams or Either of them of Pitsylvania County and State of Virginia
impowering them to take the answer of the said Defendant.

Alexr Nelson - compt.)
    vs   )   Bill and Injunction
Philip North - Deft.)

For reasons appearing it is ordered by the Court that this Cause be continued
untill the next Term, and that a commission issue to Alexr Sinclair and
Jacob Swoope of Augusta County and State of Virginia, impowering them or
either of them to take the answer of the Defendant Philip North.

James Berry - Compt.)
    vs   )   Bill and Injunction
Richard Mitchell & others)

On the 15th day of March this Cause came on to be heard, Bill and answer
being read, it was thereupon ordered by the Court that the Injunction of the
Complainant be Dissolved.

(p-192) David Russell - compt.)
       vs   )   Original Bill
    John Gass - Deft.)

For reasons appearing it is ordered by the Court that this Cause be continued
and that Defendant have time untill next Term to file his answer.

William Vannerson agent for) - Compt.)
David Ross   )   )
    vs   )   Bill & Injunction
Michl Montgomery &) Defts.)
William McCormick)   )

On reading the bill of the complainant, and the Defendants, having
demured thereto, on motion to argue the demurer the Court were of opinion
that they have time to argue untill next term; on motion the demurer was
withdrawn at the costs of the parties demuring, and the answers of the de-

fendants ordered to be filed; and on reading the Bill and the Answers the
Court ordered that the Injunction of the complainant be Dissolved, on motion
of the complainants attorney it is also ordered by the Court that the answer
of Michael Montgomery be refered to the Clerk & Master in Equity for his
report, whether any and if any, what costs the Defendant   (p-193) Michael
Montgomery should be taxed with for superpluouse and impertinent matter in
his answer.

John Johnston - compt.)
    vs   )   Bill and Injunction
Samuel May - Deft.)

On the 15th day of March this cause came to be heard, Bill and Answer being
read it was thereupon ordered by the Court that the Injunction of the complainant be Dissolved and bill dismiss'd.

Thomas Ross - compt.)
    vs   )   Bill and Injunction
Samuel Vance - Deft.)

For reasons appearing it is ordered by the Court that this cause be continued
and that the Defendant have time untill next term to answer.

Samuel Wilson - compt.)
      vs   )   Bill and Injunction
Jonathan Langdon &) Defts.)
John Tillery   )   )

On the 15th this cause came on to be heard, Bill and Answer being read it is
ordered by the Court that the Injunction of the complainant be Dissolved.

(p-194)   Robert Campbell - compt.)
                vs   ) Original Bill
           Thomas Gibbons - Deft.)

This cause continued by consent untill the next Term for the Answer of Thomas
Gibbons the Defendant.

Thomas Berry - compt.   )
    vs   )   Bill and Injunction
Lucy Amis Executrix of) - Deft.)
Thomas Amis deceased)   )

In this Cause the defendant filed a plea in abatement and on argument of
Counsel for complainant and defendant, the Court were of opinion that the
plea in abatement be Sustained.

Robert McAfee   )
    vs   )   Scricrifacias for costs
Simon Kerkendall)   sheriffs return not Executed by reason of the death of
the Defendant.   Jas Cage D.

The Court order that Sci fa issue against the heirs and legal representatives
of the said Simon Kirkindall decd.

(p-195) Samuel Harris
    vs
  John Newman Ex. &   )
  Margaret Hays Exectx of) Sceirefacias for costs
  Charles Hays decd.   )

 The sheriff's return as follows (to wit) made known to both defendants in presence of Thomas Kennedy & Robt. Gray Feby. the 21st 1800.
              Chris Conway D.p
The Defendants
Being solemnly called, and failed to appear the Court do order that Judgment be Entered up against them according to Sci fa.

Garret Fitzgerrald &)
Benjamin Ford   ) Scierfacias for costs
   vs.   ) made known in
James English   ) presence of Thos. Kennedy
         & Robt. Gray Feby, 21st 1800.
           Chris Conway D. p
The defendant
Being Solemnly called and failed to appear the court do order that Judgment be Entered up against him according to Sci fa.

(p-196)   SEPTEMBER TERM 1800

 At a Court of Equity begun and held in the State of Tennessee for the District of Washington in the Town of Jonesborough on the Eleventh day of September 1800.

     Present the Honorable
    Archibald Roane) Esquires
    David Campbell &) Judges
    Andrew Jackson) this Court

Henderson & Company - compts.)
   vs   ) Original Bill
Henderson & Company - Defts.)

 Ordered by the Court that this Cause be continued untill the next Term for a Decree.

William Gardner - compt.)
   vs   ) Original Bill
Mary Looney & the heirs of)- Defts.)
Benjamin Looney decd.))

 Decree made up, and ordered by the Court to be Enroled.

John Carney - compt.   )
   vs   ) Original Bill
Ephraim Dunlop & the) - Defts.)
Heirs of Ann Moore Decd.))

On the Eleventh day of September this (p-197) cause came on to be heard,

when also came a Jury (to wit) James Gordon, James Armstrong, Andrew English
James Penny, Richard Mitchell, Robt. Allen, Archibald Williams, Pendexter
Pain, James McClain, George Roberts, Andrew Greer and John Bayless, who being
impanneled and sworn to well and truly try the following issues of fact (to
wit) whether Ann Moore Signed and delivered the instrument of writing Stated
in the Complainants Bill to the Complainant – and if she did either by her
self or her attorney legally authorized, – whether any, and if any, what consideration was paid by the complainant to the said Ann Moore for the Same;
on their oath do say: we find that Ann Moore did not Sign nor deliver the
instrument of writing Stated in the complainants bill by herself or her legal
attorney and we further find that no consideration was paid by the complainant
to Ann Moore for the Same – where upon the Court do order that the Bill of
the Complainant be Dismissed with Costs.

(p-198) Robert Keer – compt.)
                vs   )   Bill and Injunction
         Alexander Meek – Deft.)

Ordered by the Court that this Cause be continued untill the next Term, and
that commissions issue to complainant and defendant.

James Berry – compt.   )
                vs   )   Bill and Injunction
Lucy Amis, Executrix of) – Deft.)
Thomas Amis decd.   )

For reasons appearing ordered by the Court that this cause be continued untill
the next Term and that commissions issue for Defendant publication of Testimony on the first day of next Term.

Cottral Bailey – compt.)
                vs   )   Retained as an original
Andrew Greer – Deft.)

For reasons appearing, ordered by the Court that this cause be continued untill
the next Term, and commissions issue for complainant and defendant. Publication of Testimony on the first day of the next Term.

(p-199) David Wright – Compt.)
                vs   )   Original Bill
         Alexander Bain – Deft.)

This cause continued at the request of the complainant.

Richard Woods – Compt.   )
                vs   )   Bill and Injunction
Batt Woods, Thomas Wood &) – Defts.)
Benjamin Gist   )   )

For reasons appearing it is ordered by the Court that this Cause be continued
untill the next term and commission issue to Compt. and defendant. Publication of Testimony on the first day of the next term, issues made up under
the directions of Court, and ordered to filed.

Ruth Brown – compt.   )
                vs   )   Bill & injunction
William Whitson Exr. of) Deft.)
John McDowell decd.   )   )

This cause continued by consent, untill the next term. The complainant and defendant do agree that the Depositions here to fore filed in this cause shall be admitted, reserving any exception to the competency of the witness, ordered by (p-200) the Court that commissions issue to the deft. Publication of Testimony the first day of the next term.

```
William Cobb  - compt.      )
        vs                  )    Original Bill
William Conway & others - defts. )
```

On the Eleventh of September this cause came to be heard bill and answer being read it is ordered by the Court to be continued for argument at the next term also ordered by the Court that a Subpoena Duces Lecum issue commanding James Sevier Clerk of Washington County Court to be and appear at the next Superior Court of Law and Equity, and bring forward before this Honorable Court the bond of John Carter original Entry taker of Washington County to be given in Evidence in the above cause.

```
Michael Harrisson  - compt. )
        vs                  )    Retained as an original
William Murphy & ) - Defts. )
Isaac Thomas     )          )
```

For reasons shown it is ordered by the Court that this cause be continued at the costs of (p-201) the complainant. Publication of Testimony on the first day of the next term.

```
John Sharp  - compt.)
        vs          )    Retained as an original
John Adair - Deft. )
```

On argument of Counsel for complainant and defendant it is ordered by the Court that the bill of the complainant be Dismissed with costs.

```
John Blevins  - compt.)
        vs            )    Retained as an original
John Shelby - Deft.  )
```

Further issues offered by the complainants attorney which was over ruled, and on argument of Counsel for compt. and defendant the Court order that this cause be continued untill the next term for a final hearing.

```
John Johnston  - compt.)
        vs             )    Bill and Injunction
Moses Carrick - Deft.  )
```

Ordered by the Court that this cause be continued, and that issues be made up at the next term.

```
(p-202)  Thomas King  - compt.          )
              vs                        )    Original Bill
         Bennoni Caldwell, Joel ) - Defts. )
         Gillenwater & John Hall )      )
```

This cause ordered to be Dismissed by Verball order of the compt.

William Christmas - compt.)
          vs   )   Original Bill
Nathaniel & Samuel) - Defts.)
Henderson   )   )

For reasons shewn it is ordered by the Court that this cause be continued
on the same rule made at the last Term.

Michael Montgomery - compt.)
      vs   )   Retained as an original
William Burke - Deft.   )

    Ordered by the Court this cause be contd untill the next term, and that
commissions issue to compt. and deft. notice to the Defendants atty. shall
be deemed sufficient in taking depositions. Publication of Testimony the
first day of the next term, the Rule made in this cause, to amend the bill
is discharged.

(p-203)   John Mileken - compt.)
             vs   )   Bill and Injunction
           John Smith - Deft.)

This cause continued by consent untill September Eighteen hundred and one.

Robert Kile - compt.   )
      vs   ) To perpetuate testimony
The Heirs of William Ingram decd. - Defts)

    Ordered by the Court that this cause be continued untill the next
term, and that commissions issue to the complainant.

John Coulter - compt.   )
      vs   )   Bill and Injunction
Richard Mitchell &) - Defts.)
Thomas Houghton   )   )

    Ordered by the Court this cause be continued untill the next term; and
that commission issue to Judge Walton and Judge Carnes of the State of Georgia
impowering them or Either of them, to Receive upon oath the answer of Thomas
Houghton and also publication be inserted in the Knoxville Gazette that
the said Thomas Houghton file his answer at the next term otherwise the bill
of the complainant will be taken pro confesso as to him.

(p-204)   William Skillern - compt.)
             vs   )   Bill and Injunction
         Nicholas Hawkins - Deft.)

Ordered by the Court that this Cause be continued untill the next term issues
made up under directions of the Court and ordered to be filed.

John Yancy - compt.)
     vs   )   Original Bill
James Reed - Deft.)

Ordered by the Court that this cause be continued untill the next term, commissions for complainant and defendant issues filed. Publication of Testimony

on the third day of the next term.

```
Mark Mitchell  -  compt.   )
          vs               )    Bill and Injunction
Michael Montgomery - Deft. )
```

On the twelfth day of September this cause came to heard, and on motion of the defendants attorney, it is ordered by the Court that the Defendant have leave to amend his answer; and the defendant amended and filed the same at this present term.

```
(p-205)   Lawrence Horn  -  compt.)
                vs                )    Bill and Injunction
        Thomas Gibbons  - Deft. )
```

For reasons appearing it is ordered by the Court, that this cause be continued untill the next term, and that commissions issue to complainant and defendant. Publication of Testimony on the first day of next term.

```
William Russell & others  - compts.       )
          vs                               )   Bill and Injunction
The Heirs of William & Richard )           )
Caswell deceased and           ) - Defts. )
     against                   )           )
Joseph Blair                   )           )
```

For reasons appearing it is ordered by the Court that so fat as the Bill of the complainants has been taken for confessed against the Heirs and legal representatives of William and Richard Caswell deceased that the same be set aside, and that the complainants have leave to amend their Bill.

```
James Reed  -  compt.   )
        vs              )    Original Bill
John Adams & ) - Defts. )
Jacob Sooman )          )
```

Answers filed, ordered by the Court that this cause be continued untill the next term and commissions issue to complainant and defendant Publication (p-206) of Testimony on the Seventh day of next term; Rule for Testimony set aside by consent and time given till next term to file a replication.

```
Robert Allen  -  compt.   )
        vs                )    Bill and Injunction
Archibald Blackburn - Deft. )
```

This cause continued by consent, untill the next term; issues made up under directions of the Court and ordered to be filed, commissions for complainant and defendant. Publication of Testimony on the first day of next term.

```
John Pitner  -  compt       )
        vs                  )   Retained as an original
Robert & Thomas Rogers - Defts. )
```

This cause continued by consent , commissions for complainant and defendant.

Robert Alison - compt.   )
                  vs   )   Original Bill
Isaac Shelby & others - Defts.)

For reasons appearing it is ordered by the Court that this cause be continued
and commissions issue for complainant and defendant issues made up under the
directions of the Court. Publication of Testimony on the Third day of next
term.

(p-207)   Thomas King - compt.)
                  vs   )   Bill and Injunction
           John Smith - Deft.)

     Ordered by the Court that the bill of the complainant be taken pro con-
fesso agreeable to a publication heretofore inserted in the Knoxville Gazette.

Alexander Nelson - Compt.)
          vs   )   Bill and Injunction
Philip North - Deft.   )

For reasons appearing it is ordered by the Court that this cause be continued
on the same rule of last term and that a publication be inserted in two successive numbers of the Knoxville Gazette, that the defendant do file his
answer on the first day of the next term otherwise the Bill of the complainant
will be taken pro confesso.

David Russell - Compt.)
       vs   )   Original Bill
John Gass - Deft.   )

For reasons shown it is ordered by the Court that this cause be continued
untill next term, and that commissions issue to complainant and defendant.
Publication of Testimony on the third day of the next term.

(p-208)   Henry Burum - Compt.   )
                  vs   )   Original Bill
           John Gold Fletcher & Others - Defts.)

     This cause dismissed by verball order of the complainant September the
8th 1800.

Thomas Ross - Compt.)
       vs   )   Bill and Injunction
Samuel Vance - Deft.)

On the 12th day of September this cause came to be heard, bill and answer
being read it is ordered by the Court that the Injunction of the complainant
be Dissolved; and on motion of the complainants attorney the bill is retained
as an original, and the defendant Samuel Vance have the benefit of his Judge-
ment at Law on his giving bond with sufficient Security in the penal sum of
one thousand dollars to refund the sum recovered by him at Law against the
complainant with legal interest, in case a Decree should be had in favour of
Richard Woods in a suit now pending in the Court of Equity, for Washington
District, wherein the said Richard Woods is complainant against Batt Wood
Thomas Wood and Benjamin Gist is Defendants.

(p-209)   Robert Campbell - Compt.)
                    vs   ) Original Bill
           Thomas Gibbons - Deft.)

For reasons appearing it is ordered by the Court that this cause be continued
and the complainant leave untill next Term to amend his bill.

Bennett Boggess - Compt.)
                vs   ) Bill and Injunction
Joseph Bates &   ) - Defts.)
James Galbreaith)   )

On the 13th of September this Cause came to be heard, bill and answer
being read it is ordered by the Court that the injunction of the complainant
be Dissolved.

John Shipley - Compt.)
           vs   ) Original Bill
James Anderson - Deft.)

Ordered by the Court that alias subpoena issue against the Defendant to
answer at the next term.

Jane Brooks - Compt.   )
           vs   ) Original Bill
Walter Keer &   )- Defts.)
Alexander Chambers)   )

(p-210)   Ordered by the Court that an alias subpoena issue against the Defendant with a copy of the bill to answer at the next term.

Stephen Wood - Compt.   )
           vs   ) Original Bill
Samuel Smith &) - Exrs. Defts.)
James Lee   )   )

Ordered by the Court that this cause be continued untill next term for
a replication.

Ephraim Dunlop
           vs
Charles Robertson &) Exrs. of Charles)   Scerifacias
James Gordon   ) Robertson decd.)
   and against   ) bail for   )
William Cox   ) Auston Shoat   )

Made known before Michael Harrisson & Jacob Gyer in the month of April
1800 - Bruce Blair Shff.

Being Solemnly call'd and failed to appear it is ordered by the Court that
Judgment be Entered according to Sceire faceas.

(p-211)   MARCH TERM 1801

At a Court of Equity begun and held in the State of Tennessee for the

District of Washington in the Town of Jonesborough on the <u>Twelvth</u> day of .
March 1801.

Present the Honorable
Archibald Roane) Esquires
David Campbell &) Judges
Andrew Jackson   ) of this Court

Henderson & Company - Compts.)
       vs   )   Original Bill
Henderson & Company - Defts.)

For reasons shown it is ordered by the Court that this cause be continued
untill the next Term for a Decree.

Robert Keer - Compt.)
     vs   )   Bill and Injunction
Alexander Meek - Deft.)

For reasons appearing it is ordered by the Court that this cause be continued
untill the next Term, and that commission issue to complainant and defendant.

(p-212)   James Berry - Compt.   )
              vs   )   Bill and Injunction
           Lucy Amis, Executrix of) - Defts.)
           Thomas Amis decd.   )   )

On argument of Counsel for complainant and defendant the Court were of opinion
that the issues of fact made up in this cause be Set a side, and the Court
do order that the injunction of the complainant be Dissolved and bill dismissed, for want of proper parties thereto, in consequence of the <u>abatment</u>
by the death of Thomas Amis, and not being revived in due time.

Cottral Bailey -- Compt.)
     vs   )   Retained as an original
Andrew Greer - Deft.)

The complainant and defendant this day came to the following compromise (to
wit) at Mutual costs <u>exceping</u> the copying of the amended bill of the complainant which the compt. agrees to pay himself, whereupon the complainant
do order this cause to be Dismissed March the 10th 1801.

David Wright - Compt.)
     vs   )   Original Bill
Alexander Bain Ɵ Deft.)

This cause continued by consent.

(p-213)   Richard Woods - Compt.   )
              vs   )   Bill and Injunction .
           Batt Wood, Thomas Wood &) - Defts.)
           Benjamin Gist   )   )

For reasons appearing it is ordered by the cour' that this cause be continued
untill the next term and that commissions issue to complainant and defendants .
Publication enlarged till the <u>Secon</u> day of next Term.

Ruth Brown - Compt.   )
   vs   )   Bill and Injunction
William Whitson Exr. of) - Defts.)
John McDowell decd.   )   )

On the thirteenth day of March this cause came to be heard, when also
came a Jury (to wit) James Penny, Andrew English, Joseph Young, David Russell
Benjamin Holland, John Collier, Julius Conner, Isaac Tipton, Samuel Smith,
John Morris, John Gass and Matthew Cox, who being impanneled and sworn well
and truly to try the following issues of fact (to wit) whether the notes or
obligations mentioned the complainants bill, were obtained from her by means
of duress by John McDowell the defendants Testator and whether Jacob Brown
deceased in his lifetime did not give (p-214) to John McDowell Land or
other property in full Satisfaction of the demands of him the said John.
On their oath say we find the notes or obligations mentioned in the complainants bill were obtained from her by means of duress by John McDowell,
the Defendants Testator, and that Jacob Brown deceased in his lifetime did
give to John McDowell Land or other property in full satisfaction of the
demand of him the said John.

William Cobb - compt.   )
   vs   )   Original Bill
William Conway & others - Defts.)

On return of the subpoena ducestecum_ for James Sevier clerk of the County
Court of Washington and on his appearance in Court it appearing that the
bond mentioned therein is not in his possession and it further appearing
that the same bond is in the possession of his Excellency John Sevier; it
is therefore ordered by the Court that an other subpoena duces te cum
issue directed to the sheriff of Knox County to summon the said John Sevier
to appear at the next Court with said bond to be given in Evidence in the
above cause.

(p-215)   Michael Harrisson - Compt.)
              vs   )   Retained as an original
          William Murphey &) - Defts.)
          Isaac Thomas   )   )

On the 14th this cause came to heard bill and answers being read the following
issues of fact were made up under the directions of the court (viz) whether
Murphey one of the defendants at the time of the execution of the Bill of
Sale in the complainants bill mentioned, knew that the said negroe man there
in named was a free man, and if he did, did he by any expression induce the
said complainant to believe that he would not consider the complainant
answerable to him Murphy one of the defendants as Security to Isaac Thomas.
Commissions for complainant publication inlarged till the third day of next
Term. Service of notice on Defendants attorney to be sufficient.

John Blevins - Compt.)
   vs   ) Retained as an original
John Shelby - Deft.)

Motion of the complainants attorney to file a Supplimentory bill, which motion
was over ruled (p-215) there being no affidavit filed or new matter shewn,
Ordered by the Court to continued, and set for hearing at the next Term.

John Johnston - Compt.)
      vs   )   Bill and Injunction
Moses Carrick - Deft.)

Publication enlarged till the first day of next Term commissions for complainant and Defendant.

William Christmas - Compt.)
      vs   )   Original Bill
Nathaniel & Samuel) - Defts.)
Henderson   )   ?

On motion of the complainants attorney it is ordered by the court that he
have leave to amend his bill, see bill; issues made up and filed under directions of the Court commissions for complainant and deft.

Michael Montgomery - compt.)
      vs   )   Retained as an original
William Burke   - Deft.)

This cause Dismissed by order of the complainant.

(p-217) John Meliken - Compt.)
          vs   )   Bill and Injunction
         John Smith - Deft.)

For reasons appearing it is ordered by the Court that this cause be continued
untill the next Term.

Robert Kile - compt.   )
      vs   )   To perpetuate
The Heirs of William) - Defts.)   Testimony
Ingram deceased   )   )

Ordered by the Court to be continued untill the next term, and commissions compt.
and defendants.

John Coulter - Compt.   )
      vs   )   Bill and Injunction
Richard Mitchell &) - Defts.)
Thomas Houghton)   )

On motion of the complainants Counsel for leave to amend the bill, and
on argument thereon the motion was discharged.

Ordered by the Court that a commission be directed to Archibald Grissum,
James Nesbitt and William Greer or either of them of Greene County and State
of Georgia to take the answer of Thomas Houghton one of the Defendants in this
cause and that the said answer be (p-218)   filed by the Second Wednesday
of the next term or the bill of the complainant will be taken pro confesso
as to the said Houghton.

William Skillern - Compt.)
      vs   )   Bill and Injunction
Nicholas Hawkins - Deft.)

On the 13th of March this cause came to be heard, when also came a Jury (viz)

Isaac White, William Blair, Samuel Dinsmore, Hudson Johnston, John Embree, Walter King, James English, Saml Vance, John Kile, Elisha Rhodes, Thomas Brown & Archibald Blackburn who being impanneled and sworn well and truly to try the following issues of fact (viz) whether William Skillern made an absolute assumsit to pay five Dollars and twenty five cents to the Defendant if he did at what time, and for what consideration.

On their oath do say we do find that William Skillern made an absolute assumsit to the Defendant of five Dollars and one quarter of a Dollar 2d. it was within one year before the said defendant brought a suit against said Skillern for the same. 3d. That it was (p-219) for said defendants proportionable part of monies arising from the Sale of certain property taken from the Cherokee Indians Colonel Arthur Campbell Commandant and the Collection and paying out of the same was placed in the hands of said Skillern for the benefit of said defendant and others -- motion by the complainants counsel for a new trial, and on argument motion over ruled, ordered by the Court to be continued and set for hearing at the next Term.

John Yancy - Compt.)
   vs   )   Original Bill   :
James Reed - Deft.)

This cause continued by consent Rule of publication enlarged to the Second day of next Term commissions for compt. and defendant.

Mark Mitchell - compt.)
   vs   )   Bill and Injunction
Michael Montgomery - Deft.)

On motion of the Defendants attorney to read bill and answer to Dissolve the complainants injunction, on bill and the amended answer of the Deft. which motion was over ruled by the (p-220) Court and ordered to be continued, and set for hearing at the next Term, commissions for complainant and defendant. Publication of Testimony on the Second day of next Term.

Lawrence Horn - Compt.)
   vs   )   Bill and Injunction
Thomas Gibbons - Deft.)

    For reasons appearing it is ordered by the Court that this Cause be continued, publication of Testimony enlarged to the first day of next term commissions for compt. and defendant notice to the complainants attorney shall be Deemed sufficient.

(p-221) William Russell & others - Compts.
               vs
      The Heirs of William &)
      Richard Caswell decd &)   Bill and Injunction
          against   )
      Joseph Blair   )

Amended Bill filed March term 1801 on motion of the complainants by their attorney, and it appearing to the satisfaction of the Court that Dullan Caswell and William R. Caswell heirs etc. of Richard William & Samuel Caswell (p-221) deceased Defendants are not inhabitants of this State. It is therefore ordered that that the said Dullan Caswell and William R. Caswell heirs as aforesaid, do appear at our next Superior Court to be held for the District of Washington in Jonesboro on the first Monday in September next and file their several answers thereto, or the bill of the complainants will be taken for confessed and that this order be twice published in the North Carolina Minerva published in Raleigh & in the Knoxville Gazette.

And that a commission issue directed to John Haywood, William White & Robert Williams Esqr. or either of them to take the answers of the said Defendants.

```
James Reed  -  Compt.   )
        vs              )     Original Bill
John Adams & ) - Defts. )
Jacob Sooman )          )
```

For reasons appearing it is ordered by the Court that this cause be continued untill the next term and that commissions issue to compt. and defendant. Publication of Testimony on the first day of next term.

```
(p-222)Robert Allen  -  Compt.     )
            vs                     )   Bill and Injunction
       Archibald Blackburn - Deft. )
```

This cause continued by consent, publication enlarged till the first day of the next term commissions for complainant and defendant.

```
John Pitner  -  Compt.          )
       vs                       )  Retained as an original
Robert & Thomas Rogers - Defts. )
```

This cause continued on the same Rule of last term, publication of Testimony the first day of next term.

```
Robert Alison  -  Compt.        )
         vs                     )   Original Bill
Isaac Shelby & others Defts.    )
```

This cause continued by consent. Publication enlarged to the 3rd day of next term commissions for compt. and defendant.

```
Thomas King  -  compt.)
     vs               )   Bill and injunction
John Smith  -  Deft.  )
```

It was moved by the Defendant by his attorney that the order for taking the bill (p-223) pro confesso should be set aside on an affidavit of Thomas Jackson which motion was over ruled, and ordered by the Court that this Cause be set for hearing exparte and Decree at next Term.

```
Alexander Nelson  -  Compt.)
       vs                  )  Bill and Injunction
Philip North      -  Deft. )
```

For reasons shown it is ordered by the Court that this cause be continued on the same rule as at September Term 1800.

David Russell - Compt.)
　　　vs 　　　　　　)　　Original Bill
John Gass　　 - Deft.)

    Ordered by the Court that commissions issue to complainant and defendant & Rule for publication inlarged till the third day of next Term.

Thomas Ross - Compt.)
　　　vs 　　　　　　)　　Bill & Injunction
Samuel Vance - Deft.)

Ordered by the Court that this cause be continued on the same rule of last term.

(p-224)　Robert Campbell - Compt.)
　　　　　　　vs　　　　　　)　Original Bill
　　　　　Thomas Gibbons - Deft.)

    For reasons shown it is ordered by the Court that time be given to answer untill the first day of next term.

John Shipley - Compt.)
　　　vs　　　　　　　　)　　Original Bill
James Anderson - Deft.)

This cause dismissed by order of the complainants attorney and James Kain assumes costs.

Jane Brooks - Compt.　)
　　　vs　　　　　　　　　)　Original Bill
Walter Keer &　) - Defts.)
Alexr Chambers)　　　　　)

The defendants not having entered their appearance agreeable to the rules of this Court; and it appearing that they are not inhabitants of this state, it is therefore ordered by the Court that publication be made twice in the Knoxville Gazette that the Defendants appear and answer with in the three first days of the next term otherwise the Bill of the complainant will be taken pro confesso.

(p-225)　Stephen Wood - Compt.　)
　　　　　　　vs　　　　　　　)　　Original Bill
　　　　　Samuel Smith &　) - Defts.)
　　　　　James Lea Exrs.)　　　　　)

    Ordered by the Court that this cause be continued and that commissions issue to complainant and defendant thirty days notice to be given for taking depositions in the State of Virginia and Georgia.

John Sevier - Compt.　)
　　　vs　　　　　　　　)　Bill & Injunction
Michael Harrisson - Deft.)

    On the 14th of March this cause came to be heard bill and answer being read the Court order the complainants injunction to be Dissolved, on the defendant giving bond with sufficient Security to refund the money should

a decree hereafter be had against him on the retention of the bill as an
original commissions for complainant and defendant.

```
Hudson Johnston &  ) - Comptss )
Joel Shropshire    )            )
     vs            )            )    Bill and Injunction
Richard Mitchell & ) - Defts.   )
Thomas Ingram      )            )
```

(p-226)   Thomas Ingram's answer filed, ordered by the court that time be
given for Mitchell's Answer till the first day of next Term.

```
Thomas Jackson - Compt.)
     vs                )    Bill & Injunction
John Honeycut  - Deft. )
```

The defendant not having entered his appearance agreeable to the rules of
this Court and it appearing that he is not an inhabitant of this State: it
is therefore ordered that publication be made twice in the impartial ob-
server published by Green in the Natchez, and twice in the Knoxville Gazette
that he do file his answer at the next term otherwise the bill of the complainant will be taken pro confesso.

```
Thomas King - compt.
     vs
John McCaughan - Deft.
```

Ordered by the Court that Alias Subpoena issue to Hawkins County.

```
(p-227)   Allen Gillespie - Compt.          )
               vs                            )    Original Bill
          Samuel Perciful & others - Defts. )
```

Ordered by the Court that time be given to answer till the Second Thursday of
next term, and it appearing that Samuel Perceful is not an inhabitant of this
State it is also ordered by the Court that publication be made twice in the
Nashville Gazette that he do appear at the next term and answer otherwise the
bill of the complainant will be taken pro confesso.

```
William P. Chester - Compt. )
     vs                      )    Bill & Injunction
John Kennedy - Deft.         )
```

This Cause abated by plea of the defendant motion for an injunction in open
Court, ordered that Writs of injunction and Subpoena issue agreeable to the
prayer of the complainant. This cause dismissed by order of the Compt.
August 1801.

(p-228)   SEPTEMBER TERM 1801

At a Court of Equity begun and held in the State of Tennessee for the
District of Washington in the Town of Jonesborough an the 17th day of September
1801.

Present the Honorable
David Campbell &) Esquires
Andrew Jackson) Judges of this Court

Henderson & Company - compts.)
    vs   )   Original Bill
Henderson & Company - Defts.)

For reasons appearing it is ordered by the Court that leave is given to
amend the bill of the complainants, agreeable to instructions filed.

Robert Keer - compt.)
    vs   )   Bill and Injunction
Alexander Meek - Deft.)

This cause continued on the same rule of last Term.

David Wright - compt.)
    vs   )   Original Bill
Alexander Baine - Deft.)

For reasons appearing ordered by the Court that this cause be continued untill the next Term.

(p-229)   Richard Woods - Compt.   )
           vs   )   Bill and Injunction
        Batt Wood, Thomas)- Defts.)
        Wood & Benjamin Gist)   )

Publication enlarged till the Second day of next Term commissions did po
issue for complainant and defendant.

Ruth Brown - compt.   )
    vs   )   Bill and Injunction
William Whitson Exr of) Deft.)
John McDowell decd.   )   )

Ordered by the Court that this cause be continued untill the next term for
final hearing.

William Cobb - Compt.   )
    vs   )   Original Bill
William Conway & others - Defts.)

The death of George Conway one of the defendants in this cause, Suggested, and
on motion of the Counsel for the complainant, it is ordered by the court
that a Scieri facias issue Against James Conway Legatee of the said George
decd to appear at the next term and revive.

(p-230)   Michael Harrisson - compt.)
           vs   )   Retained as an origl
      William Murphey &) - Defts.)
      Isaac Thomas   )   )

This cause continued untill the next by consent of both parties.

```
John Blevins  -  Compt.)
        vs            )      Retained as an original
John Shelby   -  Deft. )
```

Ordered by the Court that this cause be continued untill the next term on the
same rule of last term.

```
John Johnston  -  Compt. )
        vs             )      Bill and Injunction
Moses Carrick  -  Deft. )
```

For reasons appearing it is ordered by the Court this cause be continued, untill the next Term, commissions did po issue to Compt. and Deft. and that
Service of notice on the Complainants attorney shall be deemed sufficient, if
it should be found on the trial that the defendant should not be an inhabitant
of this State.

```
(p-231)  William Christmas  -  Compt.           )
                    vs                          )  Original Bill
              Nathaniel & Samuel Henderson - Defts. )
```

Ordered by the Court that this cause be continued for hearing at the next
Term.

```
John Milekin  -  Compt.)
      vs            )      Bill & Injunction
John Smith  -  Deft.  )
```

Ordered by the Court that this cause be continued for hearing at the next
Term.

```
Robert Kile  -  Compt.           )
        vs                       )      To perpetuate Testimony
The Heirs of William ) Defts. )
Ingram Decd.          )         )
```

Continued till next Term commissions for complainant.

```
John Coulter  -  Compt.          )
      vs                         )
Richard Mitchell & ) - Defts. )
Thomas Houghton    )          )
```

On motion of the Defendants Counsel for   (p-232)   further time for Thomas
Houghton to file his answer, it is ordered by the Court for reasons appearing
to them that the said Houghton have untill the Second Wednesday of the next
Term to file his answer and that a commission issue to Archibald Grissum
James Nesbit and William Greer of the County of Greene and State of Georgia
or either of them to receive upon oath the answer of the said Thomas Houghton
or the bill of the complainant will be taken for confess'd as to him.

```
William Skillern  -  Compt.)
        vs              )      Bill and Injunction
Nicholas Hawkins  -  Deft. )
```

Ordered by the Court that this cause be continued till next Term for final
hearing.

```
John Yancy  -  Compt.)
        vs           )    Original Bill
James Reed  -  Deft. )
```

For reasons appearing it is ordered by the Court that this cause be continued
untill the next Term.

```
(p-233)   Mark Mitchell  -  Compt.  )
                 vs                 )    Bill and Injunction
          Michael Montgomery - Deft. )
```

This cause continued untill the next Term on affidavit of the complainant.
Publication enlarged till the third day of next Term commissions did po issue
for complainant.

```
Lawrence Horn  -  Compt.)
        vs              )    Bill and Injunction
Thomas Gibbons -  Deft. )
```

For reasons appearing, it is ordered by the Court that this Cause be continued
till next term, and that commissions did po issue to complainant and defendant. Publication enlarged till the third day of next term; Service of
notice on the complainants Counsel shall be deemed Sufficient, and by consent
of parties by their attorntes, the depositions of William Hord taken Since
last term shall be read on hearing this Cause without proving Notice.

```
William Russell & others  -  Compt.)
        vs                         )    Bill and injunction
Joseph Blair & others  -   Defts.  )
```

For reasons shewn, and it appearing that William R. Caswell and others the
heirs of William (p-234)   Richard & Samuel Caswell deceased are not inhabitants of this State; it is therefore ordered by the Court that publication
be inserted twice in the news paper and Washington Advertiser that the said
William R. Caswell and others the heirs as aforesaid, do appear at the next
Term and file their Several answers to the bill of the complainants otherwise, it will be Taken for confessed as to them; and that a commission issue
to John Haywood Robert Williams and William White or either of them, of
Wake County and State of North Carolina impower them or either of them to
Receive upon oath the answers of the said defendants.

```
James Reed  -  Compt.  )
        vs             )    Original Bill
John Adams & ) - Defts. )
Jacob Sooman )         )
```

Ordered by the Court that Rule of Publication be enlarged to the fourth day
of the next Term; and commissions issue to the complainant.

```
(p-235)   Robert Allen  -  Compt.    )
                 vs                  )    Bill and Injunction
          Archibald Blackburn - Deft. )
```

Ordered by the Court that this cause be continued till the next Term.

John Pitner - Compt.   )
           vs   )   Retained as an original
Robert & Thomas Rogers - Defts.)

Ordered by the Court that this Cause be continued, and that publication be enlarged to the first day of next Term, commissions to issue for complainant and defendant.

Robert Alison - Compt.   )
           vs   )   Original Bill
Isaac Shelby & others - Defts.)

Ordered by the Court that this cause be continued on the Same rule of last Term.

Thomas King - Compt.)
          vs   )   Bill and Injunction
John Smith - Deft.   )

Ordered by the Court that this cause be continued on the same rule of last Term.

(p-236)   Alexander Nelson - Compt.)
                  vs   )   Bill & Injunction
              Philip North - Deft.   )

Ordered by the Court that the Bill of the complainant, be taken for confess'd agreeable to a publication heretofore made in the Knoxville Gazette.

David Russell - Compt.)
          vs   )   Original Bill
John Gass   - Deft.)

For reasons appearing to the Court it is ordered that this cause be continued and that publication of Testimony be enlarged to the fourth day of the next Term, also commissions issue for complainant and Defendant.

Thomas Ross - Compt.)
         vs   )
Samuel Vance - Deft.)

This cause continued on the same rule of last Term.

(p-237)   Robert Campbell - Compt.)
                 vs   )   Original Bill
              Thomas Gibbons - Deft.)

Ordered by the Court that this cause be continued untill the next term, for replication.

Jane Brooks - Compt.   )
         vs   )   Original Bill
Walter Keer &) - Defts.)
Alexr Chambers)   )

For reasons appearing it is ordered by the Court that a publication be inserted

twice in the news papers and Washington Advertiser that the Defendants do
file their answers by the third day of the next Term, other wise the bill
of the complainant will be taken for confess'd.

```
Stephen Wood  -  compt.    )
Saml Smith &   ) - Defts.  )    Original Bill
James Lee Exrs.)           )
```

March Term 1801, on motion of the Defendants by their attorney it is ordered
by the Court that the complainant give Security for the costs of this suit
at the next term otherwise his bill will   (p-238)   be Dismissed — September Term 1801. On motion of the Defendants attorney, the complainants
Bill is dismissed for want of Security being given agreeable to the above
order. But the Dismission is not to prejudice the complainants claim.

```
John Sevier  -  Compt.    )
    vs                    )    Retained as an original
Michael Harrisson - Deft. )
```

Ordered by the Court that this cause be continued till the next Term.

```
Hudson Johnston &            )
Joel Shropshire - Compts.    )
    vs                       )    Bill & Injunction
Richard Mitchell & ) - Defts.)
Thomas Ingram      )         )
```

On the 18th of September this cause came to be heard the complainants bill
and the Defendants answers being read; on motion of the Defendants attorney
to Dissolve the complainants Injunction; It is ordered by Court to be continued
on an advisare untill the next Term.

```
(p-239)   Thomas Jackson  -  Compt. )
              vs                     )    Bill and Injunction
          John Honeycutt - Deft.     )
```

For reasons appearing it is ordered by the Court that this cause be continued
and that a publication be twice inserted in the Knoxville Gazette, that the
Defendant do file his answer by the Second Monday of the next Term, otherwise
the Bill of the complainant will be taken pro confesso.

```
Thomas King  -  Compt.  )
    vs                  )    Bill and Injunction
John McCaughan  -  Deft.)
```

The Defendants John McCaughan not having entered his appearance agreeable to
the rules of this Court, and it appearing that he is not an inhabitant of this
State; It is therefore ordered by the Court that a publication be twice made
in the Nashville Gazette that he do appear within the three first days of the
next Term and file his answer, other wise the Bill of the complainant will
be taken pro confesso.

```
(p-240)   Allen Gillespie  -  Compt.            )
              vs                                )    Origl Bill
          Samuel Percifield & others - Defts.)
```

It appearing to the Satisfaction of this Court that Samuel Percifield one of the Defendants in this cause; is not an inhabitant of this State; it is therefore ordered that a publication be twice made in the newspaper and Washington Advertiser published in Jonesborough, that the said Samuel Percifield do file his answer on the third day of next Term otherwise the bill of the complainant will be taken pro confesso.

```
Moses Humphreys  -  Compt.)
        vs               )   Bill and Injunction
Armsted Blevins  ê Deft. )
```

Ordered by the Court that the Defendant have untill the Seventh day of next Term to file his answer

```
John Russell  -  compt.)
        vs             )   Bill and Injunction
Roger Barton  ê Deft.  )
```

On the 18th of September this cause came to be heard, bill and answer being read It is ordered by the court the Injunction of the complainant be Dissolved on motion of   (p-241)   the complainants attorney to retain the bill as an original time is given untill the next Term to reply.

```
Ephraim Willson  -  Compt.)
        vs                )   Bill and Injunction
Samuel Vance     -  Deft.  )
```

Ordered by the Court that the Defendant have untill the next term to file his answer.

```
James Gordon &             )  - Compts. )
Charles Robertson Exrs.)             )
        vs                           )   Bill and Injunction
Thomas Gillespie  -  Deft            )
```

On the 18th of September this cause came to be heard Bill and Answer being read; It is ordered by the Court that the Injunction of the Complainants be Dissolved for one hundred & forty four Dollars Sixteen cents and the Injunction be held up as to the residue till final hearing - replication filed, commissions Did po for compt. and Defendant.

```
(p-242)   Ephraim Dunlop & the  )
          Heirs of Ann Moore Decd)   Sci fa
                    vs
          Michael Harrisson &)
          John Johnston      )
```

July the 13th 1801 made known to Michael Harrisson in presence of John Kennedy & John Irwine. John Johnston not found in the County.
                              Joseph Brown D p
Ordered by the Court that Judgment according to Scieri facias be Entered against Michael Harrisson.

```
Waightstill Avery  -  Compt. )
        vs                   )   Original Bill
James Holland  -  Deft       )
```

On motion and affidavit filed, it is ordered by the Court here, that a publication be twice made in the newspaper and Washington Advertiser published in Jonesboro and also twice in the North Carolina Mercury published at Salisbury that the Defendant James Holland do appear   (p-243)   and answer the bill of the complainant at the next Term of this Court otherwise the same to be taken pro confesso.

Ordered by this Honorable Court that William Payne Junr. be and is hereby nominated and appointed commissioner of affidavits for the County of Hawkins.

MARCH TERM 1802

At a Court of Equity begun and held in the State of Tennessee for the District of Washington in the Town of Jonesborough on the 8th day of March 1802.

Present the Honorable
David Campbell) Esquires
Andrew Jackson) Judges of this
Hugh L. White)   Court

Richard Woods - Compt.)
    vs   )   Bill and Injunction
Batt Wood, Thomas Wood))
& Benja Gist- Defendants))

Publication

(p-244)   Publication enlarged until the Second day of next Term commissions for Complainant and Defendant, and comtinued.

Michael Harrison - Complainant)
    vs   )   Retained as an original
William Murphy &   )
Isaac Thomas - Defendans   )

Ordered by the Court that this cause be continued until next Term and that commissions Issue for complainant. Publication of Testimony until the third of next Term:

John Johnston - Complainant)
    vs   )   Bill and Injunction
Moses Carrick - Defendant   )

(p-245)   Jane Brooks - Compt.   )
              vs   )   Original Bill
          Walter Keer and) Defents)
          Alexr Chambers)   )

This cause dismissed by verbal order of the complainant.

John Brown - Complt.)
    vs   )   Bill and Injunction
Nathl Davis - Defendt.)

This cause dismissed by the complainant in person.

John Yancey - Complainant)
      vs   )   Original Bill
James Reed - Defendant·)

    On the eighth day of March this cause came on to be heard before the
Honorable David Campbell and Andrew Jackson, the complainants Bill and Defendants Answer being read and the Several Issues made up thereon; came on
to be tried. It was moved by the complainants Counsel to strike out the
first Issue; and argument thereon It was ordered by the Court that he take
nothing by his motion whereupon came a Jury to wit   (p-246) William Paine,
William Delaney, Walter King, Benjamin McNutt, James Gordon, William Smith,
John Russell, William Dinwiddie, David Tate, Giles Perman, Richard Mitchell
and Robert Wily who being impannalled and Sworn well and truly to try the
following Issues of fact Viz.

first. Whether Robert Sevier mentioned in the complainants Bill purchased
Lot No, thirty one in the Town of Jonesborough as stated in the complainants
Bill, and if so, in what manner did he purchase and at what time.

Second Issue. Did John Yancy purchase said Lot number thirty one from said
Rober Sevier as Stated in the complainants Bill, or in what manner did he
purchase.

Third Issue. Did Francis Baker purchase from the complainant Said Lot, and
if he did at what time, and for what consideration, and upon their oaths do
say. We find that Robert Sevier did not purchase Lot number thirty one as
Stated in the complainants Bill. Second, we find that John Yancey that
John Yancey did not purchase Lot number thirty one from Robert Sevier, as
Stated in the complainants Bill.

(p-247) Third Issue.
               We find that Francis Baker did not purchase said Lot
from the complainant.

Court adjourned untill Tomorrow nine o'clock.

                        David Campbell
                        Andrew Jackson
                        H. L. White

Tuesday March the 9th
                Court met according to adjournment.

Richard Woods - Compt.   )
        vs   )   Bill and Injunction
Batt Wood, Thomas Wood &) Defts.)
Benjamin Gist   )   )

Publication till the Second day of next Term commissions Did po. for Compt.
and Defendant ordered by the Court to be continued.

(p-248). Michael Harrison - Compt.)
             vs   ) Retained as an origl
       William Murphy &)- Defts.)
       Isaac Thomas   )   )

For reasons shewn it is ordered by the Court that this cause be continued and

and that commissions Did po. issue to the complainant. Publication of Testimony on the third day of next Term.

Robert Allison - Compt.)
      vs   )   Original Bill
Isaac Shelby & others)

This cause continued by consent, commissions Did po. for complainant and Defendant. Publication of Testimony enlarged till the Third day of next term.

Robert Allen - Compt.)
      vs   )   Bill and Injunction
Archibald Blackburn - Deft.)

On the 9th of March, this cause came on to be heard the Bill and answer being read; and on motion of the Defendants Counsel to dismiss the complainants Bill continued for argument.

(p-249) William Christmas - Compt.)
              vs   )   Original Bill
        Nathl & Saml Henderson - Defts.)

Rule to shew cause why the Depositions taken for the complainant Should not be quash'd for want of notice being personally Served. The Court adjourn untill Tomorrow 9 o'clock.

                    David Campbell
                    Andrew Jackson
                    H. L. White

Wednesday the 10th March 1802
    The Court met according to adjournment.

              Present the Honorable
                  David Campbell)   Esquires
                  Andrew Jackson &)   Judges of this
                  Hugh L. White   )   Court

Robert Allen - Compt/   )
      vs   )   Bill & Injunction
Archibald Blackburn - Deft.)

On the motion made yesterday by the Defendants Counsel to dismiss the complainants bill, and on argument thereon before the Honorable David Campbell and Andrew Jackson   (p-250)   the Court were divided, and motion Lost.

Ordered the Defendant may have every advantage after the trial of the Issues in this cause that he would have taken by moving to set them aside or otherwise disposing of them. Whereupon came a Jury Viz. Willaim Paine, William Delany, Walter King, Benjamin McNutt, Jonathan Tipton, William Smith, Robert Allison, Moses Humphreys, David Tate, Giles Parman, John Blair, and Robert Wyley, who being impanneled and sworn to try the following issues of fact, first. whether the Defendant Executed the Bond mentioned in the complainants Bill, or not, and if he did. Second, on what Consideration the said Defendant executed said Bond upon their oaths do say, we find that the Defendant did not execute the Bond mentioned in the complainants Bill. Rule to show cause why a new trial shall not be granted.

John Squibb being summoned as a witness for the complainant Robert
Allen in the foregoing (p-251) cause being Solemnly called and failing
to appear and give Testimony as he was bound to do. It was therefore ordered
by the Court that he forfeit according to Act of Assembly and that Sci fa
Issue against the said John Squibb to appear at our next Court to shew
cause if any he can why said forfeiture shall not be made absolute.

John Pitner - Compt.   )
       vs   ) Retained as an original
Robert & Thomas Rogers - Defts.)

This cause Dismiss'd by Verball order of the complainant in person, March
the 10th 1802.

Ordered by the Court that Peter Range be fined Two Dollars and fifty cents
for his non attendance and refusing to Serve as a Juror, when Summoned and
called by the Sheriff.

Court adjourned untill Tomorrow nine o'clock.   David Campbell
                                                       Andrew Jackson
                                                       H. L. White

(p-252)   Thursday 11th of March 1802

      The Court met according to adjournment.

                        Present the Honorable

                        David Campbell)   Esquires
                        Andrew Jackson)   Judges
                        Hugh White   )   of this Court

Court adjourned untill Tomorrow nine o'clock.

                        David Campbell
                        Andrew Jackson
                        H. L. White

      Friday March the 12th 1802

      The Court met according to adjournment. Present the Honorable
                        David Campbell)
                        Andrew Jackson)   Judges in
                        H. L. White   )   Equity

(p-253)   William Christmas - Compt.   )
                  vs   ) Original Bill
           Nathl & Saml Henderson - Defts.)

On argument of the Rule to shew cause why the Depositions taken for the
complainant should not be quashed for want of notice being personally Served
and after considerable argument thereon, The Defendants Counsel moved for and
obtained leave to withdraw his motion -- Commissions for compt. and Deft.
Thirty days notice for taking Depositions in the State of North Carolina and

Kentucky.

John Coulter - Compt.   )
     vs   )   Bill & Injunction
Richard Mitchell &) Defts.)
Thomas Houghton   )   )

The answer of Thomas Houghton being presented to the Court and prayed to be
filed, and on argument whether it should be received or not by the Counsel
on both sides the Court determined that it should be received and filed.

On motion of the Defendants Counsel to take up the Defendants Answers to
Dissolve the complainants injunction and after considerable argument thereon
the Court ordered it to be continued on an advisare untill Tomorrow.

(p-254)   Henderson & Company - Compts.)
                 vs   )   Original Bill
           Henderson & Company - Defts.)

Ordered by the Court this cause be continued untill next Term, leave to
amend the bill agreeably to instructions filed.

Robert Keer - Compt.)
    vs   )   Bill & Injunction
Alexr Meek - Deft.)

This cause continued untill the next Term.

David Wright - Compt.)
    vs   )   Original Bill
Alexr Baine - Deft.)

     Ordered by the Court that this cause continued till the next Term.

Ruth Brown - Compt.
    vs
William Whitson Exr of)   Bill & Injunction
John McDowell Decd.   )

Ordered by the Court to be continued untill the next Term for a Decree.

(p-255)   William Cobb - Compt.   )
               vs   )   Original Bill
          William Conway & others - Defts.)

The death of William Conway one of the Defts in this cause Suggested, ordered
by the Court that a Scieri facias issue against the heirs and representations
to appear at next Term and revive.

John Blevins - Compt.)
    vs   )   Retained as an original
John Shelby - Deft.)

Ordered by the Court that this cause be continued untill next Term for
final hearing.

John Johnston - Compt.)
            vs   ) Bill and injunction
Moses Carrick - Deft.)

Ordered by the Court this cause be continued on the same rule of last Term,
and publication of Testimony on the Second day of next Term.

(p-256) John Meliken - Compt.)
              vs   ) Bill & Injunction
         John Smith   - Deft.)

This cause continued on the same rule of last Term. Robt

Robert Kile - Compt.   )
         vs   )   To perpetuate
The Heirs of William) Defts.)   Testimony
Ingram Decd   )   )

Continued on the same rule of last Term.

William Skillern - Compt.)
       vs   ) Bill and Injunction
Nicholas Hawkins - Deft.)

Ordered by the Court that this cause be continued untill next Term for final
hearing.

John Yancy - Compt.)
        vs   )   Original Bill
James Reed - Deft.)

On motion of the Defendants attorney ordered by the Court the complainants bill
of complaint be Dismissed with costs.

(p-257) James Reed - Compt.)
              vs   )   Original
         John Adams &) Defts.)
         Jacob Sooman)   )

This Cause dismissed by consent, each party paying their own costs agreeably
to an award filed.

Robert Allen - Compt.   )
       vs   ) Bill and Injunction
Archibald Blackburn - Deft.)

Ordered by the Court that this cause be Dismissed at the costs of the
complainants with out prejudice.

        The Court adjourned untill Tomorrow Eight o'clock.

                          David Campbell
                          Andrew Jackson
                          H. L. White

(p-258)   Saturday 13th of March 1802 The Court met according to adjournment.

Present the Honorable
David Campbell) Judges
Andrew Jackson) in
Hugh White) Equity

John Coulter - Compt.   )
          vs   )   Bill and Injunction
Richard Mitchell &)- Defts.)
Thomas Houghton   )   )

On the motion made yesterday to take up the Defendants answers to Dissolve the complainants Injunction, the Defendants Counsel moved and obtained
leave to withdraw the motion, and then moved to Dismiss the Compts. Bill
for want of Sufficient matter of Equity, and after argument against such
motion being made at this stage of the cause, the court took time to advise
and the motion to be continued to next Term with out prejudice to the pro-
gression of this cause to a final hearing.

(p-259)   Mark Mitchell - Compt.   )
                  vs   )   Bill and Injunction
           Michael Montgomery - Deft.)

This day the foregoing cause came on to be heard before the Honorable David
Campbell and Andrew Jackson bill and answer being read ordered by the Court
to be continued untill next Term for further argument.

William Russell & others - compts)
          vs   )
Joseph Blair & others   - Defts.)

This cause came on to be heard before the Honorable David Campbell
& Andrew Jackson the complainants Bill, and the demurrer of Dullam Caswel
being read, and after argument thereon, It is considered by the Court that
the Demurrer be over ruled.

And ordered that a commissions Issue to John Haywood , William White
and Robert Williams of Wake County in the State of North Carolina impowering
them or either of them to receive an oath the answer of Dullam Caswell to
such parts of the complainants Bill as has not been answered.

(p-260)   It appearing to the Court that William R. Caswell and others
the heirs of William Richard Caswell and Samuel Caswell deceased, have not
entered their appearance agreeable to a publication made at last Term in
the newspaper and Washington Advertiser. It is therefore ordered by the
Court, that the complainants Bill be taken for confessed as to them.

Thomas King - Compt.)
      vs   )   Bill & Injunction
John Smith - Defendant)

This cause came on for final hearing and on reading the complainants
Bill It is ordered by the Court that the Bill of the complainant be dismissed with costs for want of Sufficient Equity.

Hudson Johnston &) Complainants)
Joel Shropshire   )   )
    vs   ) Bill & Injunction
Richard Mitchell &) Defendants)
Thomas Ingram   )   )

On motion of the Defendt. by their Counsel to take up the answers and
disolve the complainants Injunction, agreeable to an advisary Taken last Term
Ordered by the Court that the   (p-261)   motion entered last Term be continued on advisari till next till next Term without prejudice, and that the
cause progress, to final hearing by consent of the parties.

Allen Gillispie - Compt.)
    vs   ) Original Bill
Samuel Piercefield - Deft.)

Ordered by the Court that this cause be continued, and that a commission
Issue to Isham Inlow and Jacob Laroc Esquires or either of them of Harden
County in the State of Kentucky to receive an oath the answer of the said
Samuel Piercifield, and the Said answer be filedby the third day of next Term,
otherwise the Bill of the complainant will be taken pro confesso.

Lawrence Horn - Compt.)
    vs   ) Bill and Injunction
Thomas Gibbons - Deft.)

Ordered by the Court that this cause be continued for hearing at the next
Term.

Alexr Nelson - Compt.)
    vs   ) Bill and Injunction
Philip North - Deft.)

This cause continued for hearing at the next Term.

(p-262)   David Russell - Compt.)
             vs   ) Original Bill
         John Gass   - Deft.)

This cause continued, publication of Testimony enlarged untill the fourth day
of next Term.

Thomas Ross - Compt.)
    vs   ) Bill and Injunction
Saml Vance - Deft.)

This cause Dismiss'd by the complainants attorney.

Robert Campbell - Compt.)
    vs   ) Original Bill
Thomas Gibbons - Deft.)

This cause continued, and plea set down for argument at next Term.

John Sevier - compt.   )
    vs   ) Retained as an original
Michael Harrisson - Deft.)

This cause continued untill the next Term.

(p-263)   Thomas Jackson - Compt.)
                vs   )   Bill and Injunction
        John Honeycutt - Deft.)

This cause continued, and it is ordered by the Court that a publication be twice inserted in the newspaper and Washington Advertiser that the Defendant do file his answer on or before the Second Monday of next Term otherwise the bill of the complainant will be taken pro confesso.

Thomas King - Compt.)
     vs   )
John McCaughan - Deft.)

The Defendant not having entered his appearance agreeable to the rules of this Court and it appearing that he is not an inhabitant of this State it is therefore ordered by the Court that a publication be twice inserted in the Nashville Gazette, that he do appear within the Three first days of next Term and file his answer, otherwise the bill of the compt. will be taken proconfesso.

(p-264)   Moses Humphreys - Compt.)
              vs   )   Bill and Injunction
        Armstid Blevins - Deft.)

On motion of the Defendants Counsel on reading the Bill and Answer to Dissolve the Injunction and on argument thereon, It is considered by the Court that the Injunction be dissolved for two hundred and fifty Dollars, and the Injunction be retained for the balance till final hearing.

Court adjourned untill Monday Eight oclock.

                       David Campbell
                       Andrew Jackson
                       H. L. White

Monday March the 15th 1802 the Court met according to adjournment.
    Present the Honorable
                David Campbell)
                Andrew Jackson) Judges in
                Hugh L. White) Equity

(p-265)   John Russell - Compt.)
              vs   )   Retained as an original
        Roger Barton - Deft.)

This cause continued untill next term commissions for complainant and Deft. Replication and issues filed.

James Gordon &   )   )
Charles Robertson) Exrs. Defts.)
       vs   )   Retained as an original
Thomas Gillespie - Deft.   )

This cause continued commissions for compt. and Deft. replication filed.

```
Ephraim Wilson  -  Compt.)
        vs              )      Bill and Injunction
Saml Vance    -  Deft.  )
```

This cause <u>refered</u> agreeable to a written agreement filed.

```
Waightstill Avery  -  Compt.)
        vs                 )      Original Bill
James Holland      -  Deft.  )
```

It appearing to the Satisfaction of the Court that publication has been made
agreeable to an order of this Court at the last Term; it is therefore   (p-266)
ordered by the Court that the bill of the complainant be taken pro confesso
commissions for the compt.

```
Michael Harrisson  -  Compt.)
        vs                 )      Bill and injunction
William Hall Junr. -  Deft.  )
```

This day the foregoing cause came on to be heard bill and answer being read,
it is ordered by the Court that the Injunction of the complainant be Dissolved, and that William Hall have the benefit of his Judgment at Law, on
motion of the compts. attorney the Bill is retained as an original.

```
Robert King  -  Compt.  )    Bill and Injunction
Thomas Pemberton -  Deft. )
```

This day the foregoing cause came on to, be heard, bill and answer being read,
on motion the counsel for the Deft. it is ordered by the Court that the injunction of the complainant be Dissolved and that the said Thomas Pemberton
have the benefit of his Judgment at Law and that the bill be Dismissed with
costs.

```
(p-267)   Daniel Hamlin  -  Compt.)
              vs               )      Bill and Injunction
          James Berry     -  Deft. )
```

This day the foregoing cause came on to be heard, bill and answer being read,
it is moved by the Defendants Counsel to Dissolve the Compt. Injunction, and
after argument thereon it is the opinion of the Court that the complainants
Injunction be Dissolved for one hundred and Seventy Eight Dollars Seventy
five cents, and the Injunction held up for the balance untill final hearing
replication filed.

Issue by order of the Court to be submitted to the Jury, of what value was
the rent of the plantation mentioned in complainants Bill, that James Berry
agreed to convey to said Compt. as Stated in said bill for the year beginning
February 1794 and for each Succeeding year untill March in the year 1801.

```
John Coulter  -  Compt.    )
        vs                 )      Bill and Injunction
Richard Mitchell & ) Defts. )
Thomas Houghton    )       )
```

Order of survey Joseph Cobb surveyor for the complainant.

123

(p.-268)   Hudson Johnston &) - Compts.)
             Joel Shropshire)   )
                  vs   )   Bill and Injunction
             Richard Mitchell &) - Defts.)
             Thomas Ingram   )   )

Replication filed order of survey of the premises in dispute William Paine
Surveyor for the compts.

James Crawford - Compt.   )
      vs   )   Original Bill
The Heirs of Charles) Defts.)
Robertson deceased   )   )

      Demurrer filed continued

Jacob & Henry Gyer - Compt.)
      vs   )   Bill and Injunction
John Tadlock   - Deft.)

Ordered to be continued, and that a publication be made twice in any newspaper or Gazette published in Lexinton in the State of Kentucky that the Defendant do appear on the first day of next term and answer the bill of the
complainant otherwise it will be taken for confessed, and that a commission
issue to Isaac Shelby and (p-269) William Crow of Mercer County in the sd
State of Kentucky impowering them or Either of them to take the answer of the
said John Tadlock on oath.

Alexr Torbett -   )
      vs   )   Sci fa
Thomas & John Hughes)

Made known to Thomas Hughes the presence of John Goodson and Isaac Shelby
November 1801.   Frances H. Gaines, Shff

John Hughes not found in Sullivan County. Francis H. Gaines, Shff.

Ordered by the Court that Judgment be Entered against the said Thomas Hughes
and John Hughes according to Scieri facias.

Rules established by the Judges of the Superior Court of Law and Equity in and
for the State of Tennessee for the regulation of the practice in the Court of
Equity for Washington District. First the rules to be held in the office of
the Clerk and Master in Equity for said District shall be held on the next
day after the rise of each Session of the said Court, unless the (p-270)
same shall happen to be on Sunday and in that case on the day then next following, and that the said rules, shall be held on the same day of each
Succeeding month unless the same should happen on a Sunday and in that case
on the next Succeeding day.

Court adjourned untill Court in Course.

                        David Campbell
                        Andrew Jackson
                        H. L. White

(p-271)   SEPTEMBER TERM 1802

At a Court of Equity begun and held in the State of Tennessee for the
District of Washington in the Town of Jonesborough on the 10th day of September 1802.

Present the Honorable
David Campbell   )   Esquires
Andrew Jackson &)   Judges of
Hugh L. White   )   this Court

Richard Woods - Compt.
                vs
Batt Wood, Thomas Wood &) Defts.
Benjamin Gist   )

James Galbreaith being summoned as a witness for the complainant Richard
Woods in the above cause & being Solemnly called and failing to appear and
give testimony as he was bound to do. It is therefore ordered by the Court
that he forfeit according to Act of Assembly - and that Sci fa issue against
the said James Galbreaith appear at our next Court to shew cause if any he
can why said forfeiture shall not be made absolute.

On the same day the foregoing cause came on to be tryed when also came a
Jury (to wit) William Carr, John Adams, Brice Blair, Brice M. Garner, Jacob
Brown, Robert Love, William Smith (p-272) Jesse Paine, Moses Humphreys,
Charles Robertson, Patrick Elliot, & Isaac White who being impannelled and
sworn to try the following issues of Fact (to wit).

1st. Was any conditional time legally made by Batt Wood and Richard Woods
or others in their or Either of their behalfs, in such a manner as to as-
certain the division line of their claims as Stated in the answer, and if
there was at what time and by whom.

2nd. Whither the Grant for the Premises as claimed by Batt Wood in his answer was obtained previous to the caviat entered against Richard Woods and
whither the grant obtained by Benjamin Gist for the premises and Land now
in dispute was obtained pending the caviat.

3rd. Had Batt Wood, disclaimed the land below Batts branch before the Survey
was made on which his grant issued or before the survey being made on which
the grant Issued to said Benjamin G.----

4th. Whether the survey of Batt Wood on which his grant issued includes the
same land mentioned in his Entry and whether the survey on which Benjamin
Gists Grant issued includes the land mentioned in the Entry upon which said
survey was made.

                    Upon their oath do say
1st. We find on the first issue that a conditional line was made between
John Wood on behalf of Batt Wood with Richard Woods in the fall year Seventeen hundred and Eighty two and (p-273) subsequent to the survey made
for Batt Wood and the same appears to be on or near one of the lines of the
survey aforesaid.

2nd. On the Second issue we find the grant to Batt Wood was Issued before the Entry of the Caviat against Richard Woods, and we do not find that the grant Issued to Benjamin Gist was obtained finding the Caviat.

3rd. On the third Issue we do not find that Batt Wood, disclaimed the land below Batts Branch before the Survey was made on which his grant Issued or before the Survey being made on which the grant Issued to the said Benjamin Gist.

4th. On the fourth and last Issu. we find the grant in the name of Batt Wood covers the land located for the said Batt on the waters of little Chuck ey and we do not find the Survey on which Benjamin Gists grant issued includes the land mentioned in the Entry upon which said Survey was made.

(p-274)   Michael Harrison - Compt.
                    vs
          William Murphey &) Defts.
          Isaac Thomas   )

On the 10th of September 1802 this cause called Issues of Fact made up by the Court and ordered to be filed.

Ordered by the Court that William Alexander be exempted from attending as a Juror the remainder of this Term on cause shewn.

          Court adjourned untill tomorrow nine o'clock.

                    David Campbell
                    Andrew Jackson
                    H. L. White

Saturday September 11th 1802
          Court met according to adjournment.
                    Present the Honorable
                         David Campbell
                         Andrew Jackson
                         Hugh L. White

(p-275)   lying on Clinch River containing five Thousand three hundred and seventy five acres and that there allotted to the heirs and assigns or devisees of Landon Carter, deceased and the heirs and assigns or devisees of Robert Lucas, deceased to be held in severaltyTen Thousand acres off the town in a of said Survey or Tract of two hundred Thousand acres.

          Given under our hands this seventeenth day of September in the year of our Lord one Thousand eight hundred and two in open Court.

Test   David Campbell
John Carter C. & M. E.   Andrew Jackson

Ruth Brown - Complainant   )
          vs   ) In Equity
William Whitson Exr   ) Defendant)
of John McDowell decd)   )

          On Thursday the 10th day of September A. D. 1802 A final decree in this cause was signed by the Honorable David Campbell and Andrew Jackson Esquires

Judges of said County in presence of Counsel on both sides the sustained
of the complainants Bill appeared to be that in the year 1786 while on her
way from South Carolina to the County of Washington she was arrested at the
suit of John McDowell since deceased who by duress compelled the complainant
to execute and deliver two promissory notes with out any valuable consideration
for the sum of one hundred pounds Virginia money each and   (p-276)   at March
Term 1795 the said John McDowell recovered Judgment thereon for the Sum of
Dollars   cents in the Superior Court for the District of Washington whereto the Defendant Set forth & answered that he furnished Jacob
Brown in his lifetime while holding a talk with a number of Cherokee Indians
at the house of the said John McDowel with a large quanity of provisions & a
few guns and for which the said Jacob Brown had promised as a compensation
thereof or two tracts of Land whereupon the Court on having Council on both
sides and the following facts having been found by a Jury Viz. That the notes
or obligations mentioned in the complainants Bill were obtained from her by
duress by John McDowell the defendants testator; and that Jacob Brown in his
life time did give to John McDowell land or other property in full satisfaction
of the demand of him the said John, Do order & decree that the complainants
injunction be made perpetual & that William Whitson Executor of John McDowell
pay costs witness our hands this 16th September A. D. 1802 in open Court.

Test   David Campbell
John Carter   Andrew Jackson

(p-277)   Michael Harrison - Compt.)
               vs   )   Retained as an original
          William Murphy &) - Defts.)
          Isaac Thomas   )   )

This cause continued by consent untill next Term.

William Christmas - Compt.   )
          vs   )   Original Bill
Nathaniel & Samuel Henderson - Defts.)

On the 11th of September 1802 the foregoing cause came to be tried when also
came a Jury (to wit) Andrew Greer, William Carr, John Adams, Brice Blair, Brice
M. Garner, Jacob Brown, Robert Love, William Smith, Thomas Vincent, James
Gregg, William Payne & Joseph McCullough who being impanneled and Sworn to
try the following issues of fact (to wit)

1st. Did the said Nathaniel Henderson deceased in his lifetime execute the
writing & contract copy where of appears annexed to the bill of exhibit No.2?

2nd. Did the complainant make any advances of money or make any other satisfaction to the said Nathaniel Hendersondeceased in his Life time towards his
the said William Christmas part of expences (p-278)   alluded to in his
Bill of complainant upon their oath do say on the first Issue we do find that
Nathaniel Henderson deceased did in his life time execute a writing of contract copy where of appears annexed to the Bill Exhibit.

No. 2. On the 2nd Issue we find that William Christmas the complainant did
not ever advance any money or render any other Satisfaction to the said
Nathaniel Henderson deceased towards the said William Christmas's part of
expences alluded to in his Bill of complainant more than a third of the land
alluded to in the obligation.

Court adjourned untill Monday nine o'clock.

> David Campbell
> Andrew Jackson
> H. L. White

Monday the 13th of September 1802 Court met according to adjournment.
Court adjourned untill Tomorrow nine o'clock.

> David Campbell
> Andrew Jackson
> H. L. White

(p-279) September Tuesday 14th 1802 Court met according to adjournment.
Present the Honorable

> David Campbell
> Andrew Jackson
> Hugh L. White

Robert Allison - Compt.)
      vs   )   Original Bill
Isaac Shelby & others - Deft.)

On the 14th of September 1802 this cause came to be tried, when also came a
Jury (to wit) Andrew Greer, William Carr, John Adams, Brice M. Garner, Jacob
Brown, Robert Love, William Smith, Jesse Payne, Thomas Vincent, Brice Blair,
Joseph McCullough, & William Payne, who being impanneled and sworn to try the
following issue of fact (to wit) whether the purchase of the said tract of
land of two hundred acres mentioned in the said Bill of complaint by the said
Elizabeth Hughs of the said Isaac Shelby as Sheriff was fraudulent or not.

    Upon their oaths do say, we find that the purchase by Elizabeth Hughs
now Elizabeth Woods was not Fraudulent.

    Court adjourned untill tomorrow nine o'clock.   David Campbell
                                                    Andrew Jackson
(p-280)   Wednesday September 15th 1802, Court met according to adjournment.
Present the Honorable

> David Campbell
> Andrew Jackson

David Hamlin - Compt.)
      vs   )   Bill & Injunction
James Berry - Deft.)

    The death of the complainant Suggested motion for the representations to
revive at the next Term.

John Russell - Compt.)
      vs   )   Retained as an original
Roger Barton - Deft.)

September the 15th 1802 This cause dismissed by the complainants attorney.

Robert Keer - Compt.)
      vs   )   Bill & Injunction
Alexander Meek - Deft.)

Ordered by the Court that this cause be continued untill next Term and that commissions Issue for complainant and Defendant, Publication of Testimony the first day of next Term.

(p-281)   David Wright - Compt.)
                vs   )   Original Bill
          Alexander Baine - Deft.)

On September the 15th 1802 this cause came on to be heard ordered by the Court that the complainants Bill be Dismissed with costs.

Richard Woods - Compt.   )
        vs   )   Bill & Injunction
Batt Wood, Thomas Wood &)- Deft.)
Benjamin Gist   )   )

On the 15th September 1802 moved by the complainants attorney, for a rule to shew cause why a new trial shall not be granted on the Issues in the above cause and on argument of council on both sides, it is the opinion of the Court that the Rule be Discharged and the cause set for hearing at the next Term.

William Cobb - Compt.   )
        vs   )   Original Bill
William Conway & others - Defts.)

On motion of the complainants attorney for an alias Sci fa to issue.

The Sci fa heretofore issued in this cause having not been returned and on argument thereon the Court were divided.

(p-282)   John Blevins - Compt.)
                vs   )   Retained as an original
          John Shelby - Deft.)

     On the 15th of September 1802 the foregoing Cause came to be heard, the complainants Bill and the Defendants answer, and the several issues heretofore found being read and argument of Counsel on both sides being heard it is ordered by the Court that the Bill of the complainant be Dismissed with costs.

Waightstill Avery - Compt.)
        vs   )   Original Bill
James Holland - Deft.   )

     On motion of the Defendant by his attorney to set aside the order made at last term for taking the Bill of the complainant pro confesso and on argument of counsel on both sides it is ordered by the Court that they will advise of this motion untill tomorrow.

Richard Woods - Compt.   )
        vs   )
Batt Wood & others - Defts.)

It is ordered by Court that the forfeiture entered up against James Galbreaith for failing to attend as a witness in the above cause be remitted.

(p-283)   Court adjourned untill Tomorrow nine o'clock.

David Campbell
Andrew Jackson
H. L. White

Thursday September 16th 1802, Court met according to adjournment.
     Present the Honorable
David Campbell
Andrew Jackson
Hugh L. White

Waightstill Avery - Compt.)
                 vs   )   Original Bill
James Holland - Deft.   )

September the 16th 1802, The motion made yesterday to set a side the order
made at last term for taking the Bill of the complainant pro confesso; came
on to be heard to day before the Honorable David Campbell, Andrew Jackson &
Hugh L. White and upon argument of the motion it is the opinion of the Court
that order pro confesso be set aside.

John Johnston - Compt.)
              vs   )   Bill and Injunction
Moses Carrick - Deft.)

Continued publication of Testimony Enlarged untill second day of next Term.

(p-284)   William Christmas - Compt.   )
                    vs   )   Original Bill
             Nathaniel & Samuel Henderson - Defts.)

On the 16th September 1802 this cause came to be heard and on motion it is
ordered by the Court to be continued and set for hearing at the next Term.

John Mileken - Compt.)
             vs   )   Bill and Injunction
John Smith   - Deft.)

On the 16th September 1802 This cause came on to be heard and for reasons appearing it is ordered by the Court that this Cause be continued and set for
hearing at next Term.

Robert Kile - Compt.   )
           vs   )   To perpetuate testimony
The Heirs of William Ingram deceased - Deft.)

     Ordered by the Court that this cause be continued untill next Term &
that commissions Issue for complainant.

(p-285)   John Coulter - Compt.   )
                    vs   )   Bill and Injunction
             Richard Mitchel &) - Deft.)
             Thomas Houghton)   )

September 16th 1802 The motion made at last Term to dismiss the complainants

Bill for want of Sufficient matter of Equity contained there in came on to day to be heard agreable to an adversari and on argument of Counsel for complainant and Defendant thereon it is ordered by the Court to be continued untill Tomorrow on adversari.

William Skillern - Compt.)
    vs   )   Bill and Injunction
Nicholas Hawkins - Deft.)

    This cause came on for final hearing and on reading the complainants Bill Defendants answer, and Several issues of fact theretofore found there on being read and on argument of Council on both sides. It is ordered by the Court that the following Issue be submitted to a Jury Viz did the complainant collect all or any part of the money arising from the sales of said property mentioned in said Bill, and what part, and how and when did he dispose of such money.

(p-286)   Mark Mitchel - Compt.   )
             vs   ) Bill & Injunction
        Michael Montgomery - Deft.)

This cause came on to be heard before the Honorable David Campbell and Andrew Jackson and on reading Bill and answer it is ordered by the Court that the Bill of the complainant be dismissed each paying their own costs in this Court untill the end of September Term 1800 and that the complainant pay all subsequent costs.

Lawrence Horn - Compt.)
    vs   ) Bill & Injunction
Thomas Gibbons - Deft.)

    This cause coming on it is ordered by the Court to be continued on affidavit complainants James Forgey being summoned as a witness in the above cause in behalf of the complainant and being solemnly called and failing to appear It is ordered by the Court that he forfeit according to Act of Assembly and that Sci fa Issue accordingly.

Robert Alison - Compt.   )
    vs   )   Original Bill
Isaac Shelby & others - Deft.)

Ordered by the Court that this cause be continued and set for hearing at next Term.

(p-287)   Alexander Nelson - Compt.)
             vs   ) Bill & Injunction
        Philip North   - Deft.)

    Ordered by the Court that this cause be continued for final hearing at next Term by consent of parties attornies.

   Court adjourned untill Tomorrow nine o'clock.

                    David Campbell
                    Andrew Jackson
                    H. L. White

Friday September 17th 1802, Court met according to adjournment.
      Present the Honorable

                              David Campbell
                              Andrew Jackson
                              Hugh L. Jackson

John Coulter - Compt.   )
        vs   )   Bill and Injunction
Richard Mitchel &)- Defts.)
Thomas Houghton)   )

      This cause came to day to be heard before the Honorable David Campbell &
Andrew Jackson agreeable to an advisari yesterday and after mature consideration
it is the opinion of the Court that the motion heretofore made for Dismissing
the complainants Bill for want of sufficient matter of Equity be discharged
because   (p-288)   the Court are of opinion that a motion to dismiss a bill
for want of Equity cannot be Revived at any time between the filing of an
answer and the final hearing of the cause.

William Russell - Compt.   )
        vs   )   Bill and Injunction
Joseph Blair & others - Defts.)

      Continued commissions for the complainant and Defendants to take Testimony.

      Ordered by the Court that twenty days notice shall be deemed sufficient for
taking Depositions in Moro District.

David Russell - Compt.)
        vs   )   Original Bill
John Gass   - Deft.)

Continued

Robert Campbell - Compt.)
        vs   )   Original Bill
Thomas Gibbons - Deft.)

This cause came on to be argued on plea in abatement and after hearing Councel
for the complainant and defendant It was ordered by the Court that the plea
in abatement be sustained and the Bill be Dismissed.

John Sevier Junr. - Compt.)
        vs   )   Retained as an original
Michael Harrison - Deft.)

Ordered by the Court that this cause be Dismissed with costs.

(p-289)   Hudson Johnston &) Compt.)
           Joel Shropshire)   )
                vs   )   )   Bill & Injunction
           Richard Mitchel &) Deft.)
           Thomas Ingram   )   )

      The motion made at last Term to dissolve the complainants Injunction and
continued on an adversari came on this day to be heard before Honorable David

Campbell the complainants Bill and Defendants Answer being read and on argument of Council on both sides ordered by the Court to be continued on advisari untill Tomorrow.

```
Thomas Jackson  - Compt. )
        vs             )        Bill and Injunction
John Honeycutt  - Deft. )
```

Continued order of publication twice in the newspaper and Washington Advertiser for the Defendant to file his answer by the second Monday of the next Term otherwise the Bill of the complainant will be taken pro confesso.

```
Thomas King   - Compt. )
        vs            )         Bill and Injunction
John McCaughan - Deft. )
```

Ordered by the Court that a publication be twice made in the Knoxville Gazette that the defendant file his answer within the three first days of the next Term otherwise the Bill of the complainant will be taken pro confesso.

```
(p-290)   Allen Gillespie - Compt.        )
                  vs                       )    Original Bill
          Samuel Percifield & others - Defts. )
```

The answer of Samuel Percifield Recived and filed.

```
Ephraim Wilson  - Compt.)
        vs              )        Bill and Injunction
Samuel Vance    - Deft. )
```

Ordered by the Court that the rule of reference be set aside. Continued untill next Term.

```
James Crawford  - Compt.                   )
        vs                                 )    Original Bill
The Heirs of Charles Roberson Becd. - Deft.)
```

This cause came on to be heard the complainants bill being read, and the defendants having demured thereto which was also read It is ordered by the Court that the Demurer of the Defendants be Sustained.

```
William Cocke  - Compt. )
        vs             )         Bill and Injunction
Armstid Blevins & ) Deft. )
James Kain        )      )
```

Continued for the answer of Armsted Blevins and alias Subpena against James Kain.

```
Robert Allen  - Compt. )
        vs             )         Sca fa
John Squibb   - Deft.  )
```

Ordered by the Court that the forfeiture made against the said John Squibb be set aside.

(p-291)   Leonard Henley Bullock & others)
                         vs   )
           Henderson & Company   )

On Friday the 17th September 1802 a final Decree in this cause was signed
by the Honorable David Campbell and Andrew Jackson esquires and is in the words
following (to wit) Be it remembered that heretofore John Williams Esquires of
the County of Granville Leonard Henly Bullocks of the same County, James Hogg
of Orange County, Thomas Hart, John Umstead and Susannah his wife & David
Hart filed their Bill in the Court of Equity for Washington District and there
in stated - That Richard Henderson late of Granville County Esquire Decease -
Nathaniel Hart late of_____ County in Virginia Gentleman Deceased William
Johnston late of Orange County merchant Deceased John Luttrell late of Chatham
County Gentleman Deceased in their lifetime that is to say in the year one
Thousand seven hundred and Seventy five together with them the said John
Williams, James Hogg, Thomas Hart, David Hart and Leonard Henly Bullock purchased of the nation of Cherokee Indians a very large and valuable tract of
land lying west of the Apalachian Mountains of which the said nation or tribe
of Indians were then possesed that is to say one eight part of the land so
purchased to the said Richard Henderson William Johnston John Luttrell John
Williams James Hogg Nathaniel Hart and Thomas Hart each respectively and to
their heirs and assigns forever and one sixteenth part of said lands so purchased to the said Leonard Henly Bullock and to the said David Hart each respectively and to their heirs and assigns forever to be held by them the said
purchasers in severally and   (p-292)   not at joint tenants (some propriatory
rights only excepted and that the said purchasers from the Indians tribe or
nation aforesaid obtained a grant for the same lands conveying the right as
aforesaid. And further that the general assembly of the State of North Carolina
in May Sessions in the year one Thousand seven hundred and eighty three taking
into consideration the benefit which had accrued to the said state by the
peaceable and secure settlements made by the Citizens of the said State on part
of said lands, which lay within the limits of said State on account of the
purchase aforesaid and also considering the great trouble and expence of the
persons so purchasing did by an Act which they then passed Grant to the said
Richard Henderson, Thomas Hart, John Williams, William Johnston, James Hogg,
David Hart, Leonard Henly Bullock, the heirs and assigns or Devisees of the
said Nathaniel Hart deceased and to the heirs and assigns or devisees of
John Luttrill Deceased and to and to Landon Carter Deceased and to the heirs
and devisees of Robert Lucas Deceased two hundred Thousand acres (being part
of the lands purchased of the Indians as aforesaid) to be laid out in one
Survey and bounded as follows (to wit) Beginning at the old Indian Town
in Powels Valley and running down Powels River not less than four miles in
width on one or both sides to the junction of Powels and Clinch River then
down Clinch River on one or both sides not less than twelve miles in width
for the aforesaid compliment of two Hundred Thousand acres, the said two
hundred Thousand acres to be divided amongst the Grantees last aforesaid in
the following manner, that is to say to the said Landon Carter and to the
Heirs and devisees of Robert Lucas - ten thousand acres at the lower end there
of and of the remainder one eighth part to the said Richard Henderson, one
eighth to the said Thomas Hart one eighth to the said John Williams, one
eighth to the said William Johnston, one eighth to the said James Hogg one
sixteenth part to the said Leonard Henly Bullock (p-293)   one sixteenth
part to the said David Hart, one eighth part to the heirs assigns or devisees
of the said Nathaniel Hart deceased and one eighth part to the heirs assigns
or devisees of the said John Luttrell deceased to hold to them their heirs and
assigns or devisees respectively forever according to the aforesaid proportions

th severally as tenants in common and not as joint tenants – and that the said Richard Henderson, William Johnston, Nathaniel Hart and John Luttrell in their lifetime (to wit) on or about the 20th day of August in the year one thousand seven hundred and seventy nine together with the complainants John Williams, James Hogg, Thomas Hart, Leonard Henly Bullock and David Hart by a certain Deed of covenant sealed with their seals and subscribed with their names respectively intending to make provision for a due and speedy partition of the lands purchased by them of the Indians as aforesaid, did contract bargain and agree among themselves and did by the same writing bind themselves their heirs Executors administrators and assigns respectively either to other, that in case of the death of either of them the said parties in the said purchase before a division of the same lands should be made that then the survivers of them should have full power and authority to make partition of the same land purchased of the Indians as aforesaid in the shares and proportions aforesaid and that the heirs or devisees of such deceased partner in case such heir or devisee should be an infant writing be bound to stand to and abide by such partition or division as much as if such heir or devisee were of full age and personally present and assenting to such division which Deed of covenant the complainants are ready to produce when required and further that the said Richard Henderson departed this life in or about the year 1785 having first made his last will and Testament in writing wherein he hath devised his part of land granted by the General Assembly as aforesaid to be sold for payment of his debts and left Richard Henderson Archebald Henderson and John Henderson his heirs his heirs and (p-294) further that Nathaniel Hart aforesaid departed this life on or about the month of July in the year one Thousand seven hundred and eighty two having first made his last will and Testament in writing wherein he hath divided his share of said lands so granted by the General Assembly as aforesaid to Nathaniel Hart – and also that the said John Luttrell departed this life in or about the year one Thousand seven hundred and eighty one having first made his last will and Testament in writing wherein he hath devised such part of the said lands granted by the General Assembly as aforesaid as belonging to him to be divided equally between his wife Susannah Luttrill – now Umstead and his Brothers Hugh and William in fee – and likewise that the said W illiam Johnston departed this life in or about the month of May in the year one Thousand seven hundred and eighty five having first made his last will and Testament in writing wherein he hath devised his part of the land so granted by the General Assembly as a foresaid to his daughter Amelia Johnston now Alemia Alves in fee – and that John Umstead and Susanna Luttrill entermarried with each other in the month _____ year _____

And that Amelia Johnston daughter and devisee of the said William Johnston intermarried with Walter Alves on or about the month of May in the year one Thousand seven hundred and eighty seven and that the said Walter Alves is yet under the age of twenty one years, that is to say of the age of Twenty years or there abouts – And that the children and devisees of Nathaniel Hart or some of them are infants under the age of Twenty one years that is to say Nathaniel who is of the age of Eighteen years, John who is of the age of fifteen years and Cumberland who is of the age of Eleven years – And that the children and devisees of the said Richard Henderson or some of them are infants under the age of Twenty one (p-295) years that is to say Archibald of the age of Twenty years Leonard of the age of Sixteen years and John of the age of ten years – And it is further stated that the said complainants are desirous to have the two hundred Thousand acres divided to there respective rights agreeable to the Act of Assembly aforesaid but by reason that the Several Infants aforesaid are Interested in the same lands and intitled to partition thereon and that the Brothers of the said John Luttrell deceased and the said Landon Carter reside out of the state that is to say Landon Carter in Washington County in the State of Virginia and the said Hugh Luttrill and William Luttrill brothers of the said John Luttrill in _____ County in the State ofGeorgia and are negligent or unwilling to make parti tition and that the heirs or devisions of Robert Lucas are also unknown to your orator -

Whereby the complainants cannot but by the aid of this Honorable Court procure a division of the same lands to be made - and further that the said John Luttrill in his lifetime convey to several persons a part or parts of his share or eighth in the lands purchased of the Indians as aforesaid but to whom or what parts of his eight the complainants do not know and the complainants believe that sales and conveyances have been made in like manner by others of the said partners in the purchase from the Indians as aforesaid by reason where of divers persons to complainants unknown may have some legal or equitable interest in the land granted by the General Assembly as aforesaid. In Consideration whereof the said complainants pray your Honors to appoint Guardians for the said Infants to answer for and take care of the rights of the said Infants respectively in the premises and to grant writs of subpoena directed to the guardians and also writs of Subpoena to be directed to the said Landon Carter and the said Hugh and William Luttrill brothers and devisees of the said John Luttrill and to the several persons when discovered who may have purchased from the said parties or any of them and the complainants   (p-296)   pray that a division and partition of the said to hundred Thousand acres granted by the Assembly as aforesaid in such shares as therein mentioned agreeable to their respective rights may be made after such manner as to your Honors may seem best and that after such partition shall be made your Honors will be pleased to make such decree therein as may be necessary and proper.

And afterwards the said Defendants having failed to plead answer or Demur to the said Bill it was taken proconfesso and appointed to be heard exparte.

And afterwards to wit at March Term one Thousand Eight hundred the said Cause coming on to be heard it was ordered adjudged and decreed that a Division and partition of the said land should be made in conformity with a Deed of partition executed by John Williams, James Hogg, Thomas Hart, Richard Bullock, Walter Alvis, Joseph Hart, John Umstead, Nathaniel Hart and Leonard Henderson original proprietors. —

And now to wit at September Term one Thousand eight hundred and two the said cause coming on to be finally heard before the Honorable the Court of Equity it is ordered adjudged and decreed that a division and partition be made and that then be allotted to John Umstead and Susanna his wife Hugh Luttrill and William Luttrill devisee of John Luttrill deceased to be held in severalty the land in lotts marked letter A and number 1, lott letter N, number 2 as designated in a plott of the said lands lying in Powels Valley which plott is annexed to the said partition Deed, and that there be allotted to Thomas Hart to be held in severalty lott number one and letter B lott number 2 and letter M as designated in the said plott of the said land in Powels Valley - and that there be allotted to Richard Henderson Archabald Henderson and John Henderson devisees of Richard Henderson deceased to be held severalty lotts number one and letter I lott number 2 and letter (p-297) C as designated in the said plott of said land in Powels Valley - And that there be allotted to Walter Alvis and Amelia his wife devisees of William Johnston deceased to be held in severalty lotts number one and Letter L

number 2 and letter D as designated in said plott of said land in Powels
Valley and that there be allotted to Nathaniel Hart heir of Nathaniel Hart.
deceased to be held in severalty lott number one and letter E lott number 2
and letter F as designated in the said plott of said Land in Powels Valley and
that there be allotted to Joseph Hart one of the heirs of David Hart deceased
and to the other heirs of David Hart Deceased to be held in severalty the North
Eastern Moity of lotts number one and Letter G number 2 and letter Q as designated in the said plotts of said land in powels valley - and that there be
allotted to Richard Bullock heir and devisee of Leonard Henly Bullock deceased
to be held in severalty the Southwestern Moitys of said two last mentioned
lotts the said two last mentioned lotts to be each divided by a line running
paralled to the line of the North Eastern End of the grant from the state of
North Carolina to Richard Henderson & Company to wit north forty five west
and that there be allotted to James Hogg to be held in severalty lotts number
one and letter H number 2 and letter P as designated in said plott of said
land in Powels Valley - and that there be allotted to John Williams his heirs
or devisees to be held in severalty lotts number one and letter O number 2
and letter K as designated in the said plott of said land each of the lotts
here in before described and allotted as aforesaid containing six Thousand
and five hundred acres - Of that part of companys land lying on Clinch River
that there be allotted to James Hogg to be held by him in severalty lotts
number one and letter A number 2 and letter C as   (p-298)   designated in
the plott of survey of said land annexed to said partition Deed - That there
be allotted to John Williams his heirs or devisees to be held in severalty
lotts number one land letter C number 2 and letter B as Designated in said
plott - That there be allotted to Nathaniel Hart heir of Nathaniel Hart deceased to be held in severalty lotts number one and letter H number 2 and
letter D as designated in said plott - That there be and hereby is allotted to
Richard Henderson Archabald Henderson and John Henderson heirs and devisees
of Richard Henderson deceased to be held in severalty lotts number one and
letter E number 2 and letter H as designated in said plott - that there be and
hereby is allotted to Joseph Hart and others heirs of David Hart the North
Eastern Moeitys of lotts number one and letter F number 2 and letter G to be
held severalty and to Richard Bullock heir of Leonard Henly Bullock to be held
in severalty the south western moeitys of the said two last mentioned lotts
to be divided each in two equal parts by lines running parallel with the line
of the - north eastern end of the said grant to Henderson & Company - That
there be and hereby is allotted to John and Susanna Umstead William Luttrill
Devisees of John Luttrill deceased to be held in severalty lotts number one
and letter D number 2 and letter A as designated in said plott - That there
be and hereby is allotted to Water Alvis and Amelia his wife daughter and
devisee of William Johnston deceased to be held in severalty lotts number
one and letter B number 2 and letter E as designated in said plott that
there be and hereby is allotted to Thomas Hart to be held in severally lotts
number one and letter G number 2 and letter F as designated in said plott
Each of the lotts here in divided.

(p-299)

Court adjourned untill tomorrow Six o'clock

                        David Campbell
                        Andrew Jackson
                        H. L. White

Saturday September 18th 1802, Court met according to adjournment.

Present the Honorable
David Campbell
Andrew Jackson
Hugh L. White

Hudson Johnston &	)	Compt.	)	
Joel Shropshire	)		)	
vs			)	Bill & Injunction
Richard Mitchel &	)	Deft.	)	
Thomas Ingram	)		)	

The motion made yesterday to **Dessolve** the complainants Injunction and continued on advisari came on today to be heard before the Honorable David Campbell and on mature deliberation it is thereupon ordered that the Injunction of the complainant be Dissolved - the complainants Bill retained as an original. Etheldred Williams appointed a Surveyor to survey the premises in dispute for the complainants.

(p-300)   Waightstell Avery Compt.)
               vs   ) Original Bill
     James Holland - Deft.)

This cause came on today to be heard the Defendant having demurred to the complainants Bill, it is ordered by the Court that the Demurrer of the Defendant be over ruled - and the defendant have untill the Second Monday of next Term to file his answer, and that a commission issue to Charles Lewis Esquire of Rutherford County and State of North Carolina impowering him to receive upon Oath the answer of the said James Holland & unless the deft. do file his answer by the Second Monday of next Term the bill of the complainant will be taken for confessed.

Robertsons Executors compts.)
           vs   ) Retained as an original
Thomas Gillespie Deft.   )

For reasons appearing it is ordered by the Court that a commission issue to the complainants to take the Deposition of Samuel May Senr. De be ne esse and that Eight days notice be given to the Defendants for taking the same -

    Court adjourned untill Court in course.

                   David Campbell
                   H. L. White

(p-301)   MARCH TERM 1803

At a Court of Equity begun and held in the State of Tennessee for the District of Washington in the town of Jonesborough the 16th March 1803

                 Present the Honorable

David Campbell	)	Esquires
Andrew Jackson	)	Judges of
Hugh L. White	)	said Court

Michael Harrison - Compt.)
       vs   )   Retained as an original
William Murphy &) Deft.)
Isaac Thomas   )   )

This cause continued by consent of parties.

William Skillern - Compt.)
       vs   ) Bill & Injunction
Nicholas Hawkins - Deft.)

This cause continued by consent of parties.

Moses Humphreys - Compt.)
       vs   ) Bill & Injunction
Armstead Blevins - Deft.)

This cause continued by consent of parties.

(p-302)   William Russell & others - compt.)
                  vs   ) Bill & Injunction
           Joseph Blair & others   - Defts.)

On the 16th day of March 1803 the foregoing cause came on to be heard when also
came a Jury to wit, William Paine, Valentine Sevier, Isaach White, Harken
Webb, William Calvert, Jacob Miller, Archibald Glascock, David Bragg, Andrew
Crockett, James Forgey, Andrew Greer and Enoch Merrisett who being impanneled
and sworn to try the following Issues of Fact 1st Whether the said Joseph
Garrett settled on the said tract of Land and made such an improvement on the
same as stated in the complainants Bill or any other improvement and if any
other what kind was it and at what time was such settlement and improvement
made. 2nd. Whether the said George Russell Father of the complainant purchased of the said Joseph Garrett his the said Garrett's right & claim to said
land by said settlement and improvement for a valuable consideration to him
the said Garrett paid as stated in the complainants Bill and if he did at what
(p-303) time was such purchase made 3rd. whether the said George Russell
deceased did take possession of said land by his Tenant and make further and
other improvements on the same as stated in the Bill of the Complainant and if
he did at that time and how long did the said George Russell deceased and those
claiming under him continue in possession of said land upon their oaths do
say 1st. Issue we find that Joseph Garrett made an improvement on said Land in
the year 1776& that he settled on the s ame in the same year and that Joseph
Garretts improvements was a <u>cabbin</u>built about 15 feet Square fence made & 2
or 3 acres cut and the brush heaped 2nd. We find that George Russell Father
to the said complainants did purchase the said land & improvement of the said
Garrett in the year 1780 for which the said Garrit received a valuable consideration from the said Russell at the same time. 3rd. We find that George
Russell deceased did take possession of said Land in the year 1776 & that he
and his Tenant was in possession untill the year 1786 & that there was further
inprovements made thereon.

(p-304)   Daniel Hamlin - Compt.)
                 vs   ) Bill & Injunction
          James Berry   - Deft.)

Whereas the death of the complainant was suggested at the last Term, and on
motion of Counsel on behalf of Rosannah Hamlin, and on producing the Letters

Testamentary granted to her by the Court of Hawkins County, by which it appears she is sole Executrix of the last Will and Testament of the said Daniel Hamlin deceased and has taken upon herself the execution thereof. It is ordered by the Court that the said Suit be and stand revived in the name of her the said Rosannah Hamlin sole Executrix of the last Will and Testament of the said Daniel Hamlin deceased.

Court adjourned untill Tomorrow nine o'clock.

David Campbell
Andrew Jackson
H. L. White

(p-305)   Thursday March 17th day 1803 -
The Court met according to adjournment.
Present the Honorable
David Campbell)
Andrew Jackson)   Esquires
Hugh L. White)

William Christmas - Compt.   )
vs   )   Original Bill
Nathaniel & Samuel Henderson - Defts.)

This day the foregoing cause came on for final hearing and after reading Bill and Answer and the Several Issues here to fore found by a Jury and after argument of Council on both sides the Court took time to advise thereon untill Tomorrow.

Robert Allison - Compt.   )
vs   )   Original Bill
Isaac Shelby & others - Defts.)

This day the foregoing cause came on for final hearing whereupon the Court took an advisari untill tomorrow.

(p-306)   Richard Woods - Compt.   )
vs   )   Bill & Imjunction
Batt Wood, Thomas Wood) Deft.)
and Benjamin Gist   )   )

This day the foregoing cause came on for final hearing and after reading Bill and Answer and the several Issues heretofore found by a Jury and after Argument of Council on both sides the Court took time to advise thereon untill Tomorrow.

Court adjourned untill tomorrow nine o'clock.

David Campbell
Andrew Jackson
H. L. White

Fryday March the 18th day 1803 -

The Court met according to adjournment.

Present the Honorable
David Campbell)
Andrew Jackson) Esquires
Hugh L. White)

(p-307)   William Christmas - Compt.   )
                              vs   )   Original Bill
          Nathaniel & Samuel Henderson - Defts.)

This cause being heard yesterday and continued on an advisari untill today.
It is ordered by the Court that a jury inquire what damages the complainant
hath Sustained by the non-conveyance of three thousand three hundred thirty
three acres and one third of an acre of Land a part of the four thousand acres
tract of Land described in the bond a copy of which is annexed to the complainants Bill.

Robert Allison - Compt.   )
          vs   )   Original Bill
Isaac Shelby & others - Defts.)

This cause being heard yesterday and continued on an advisari untill today.
It is thereupon ordered by the Court, that the Bill be dismissed as to Elizabeth Hughs one of the Defendants, with costs, that it be dismissed as to
Isaac Shelby another of the Defendants, the complainant and Shelby each paying
their own costs, and that a decree pass against William Hughs the other Defendant for the sum which the Judgment at Law Robert Allison against him was
credited for, by virtue of the sale   (p-308)   and receipt of the said Robert
Allison and the return of the Sheriff on the execution under which he sold the
Land of the said Hughs mentioned in the bill and that the complainant pay all
costs except those to be taxed against Isaac Shelby one of the Defendants and
that a Decree be made accordingly.

Richard Woods - Compt.   )
          vs   )   Bill & Injunction
Batt Wood Thomas Wood) Defts.)
& Benjamin Gist   )   )

This cause being heard yesterday and continued on advisari untill today. It
is thereupon ordered by the Court that a Decree be made declaring the grant
to Batt Wood mentioned in complainants Bill so far as it covers lands included within complainants Claim as described in his Bill to be void and of
no effect and also declaring that the grant to Benjamin Gist stated in said
complainants bill, so far as it covers Land included in the said complainants
claim by Entry described in his Bill as aforesaid, be void and null and that
an order be certified from this Court to the Secretary of the State of North
Carolina or proper officer authorized to Issue such warrant, authorising
(p-309)   and Directing a warrant to Issue to complainant for said land
according to his entry that a grant may Issue to him thereon.

John Johnston - Compt.)
          vs   )   Bill & Injunction
Moses Carrick - Deft.)

This day the above cause came on for final hearing and on Reading Bill and
Answer. It is ordered by the Court that the Bill of the complainant be Dismissed with costs.

John Melekin - Compt.)
       vs   )   Bill & Injunction
John Smith   - Deft.)

Ordered by the Court that this cause be continued.

John Coulter - Compt.   )
       vs   )   Bill & Injunction
Richard Mitchel &) Defts.)
Thomas Houghton   )   )

This day the above cause came on for final hearing, and on reading complainants Bill and Defendants Answers and on argument of Council on both sides. It is ordered by the Court that the bill of the complainant be dismissed with costs without prejudice.

(p-310)   Alexander Nelson - Compt.)
             vs   )   Bill & Injunction
         Phillip North   - Deft.)

This day the above cause came on for final hearing, and for reasons appearing to the Court. It is ordered to be continued untill next Term.

David Russell - Compt.)
       vs   )   Bill & Injunction
John Gass   - Deft.)

This day the above cause came on for final hearing and on reading the complainants Bill and the Defendants Answer, and on argument of Council on both sides. It is ordered by the Court that the Bill of the complainant be dismissed with costs.

James Crawford - Compt.   )
       vs   )   Original Bill
Robertsons Executors - Defts.)

This cause continued by the consent of the complainant and Defendant attorneys and leave given by the defendants attorney to the complainants to amend the Bill.

(p-311)   Hudson Johnston &) - Compts.)
         Joel Shropshire   )   )
            vs   )   Bill & Injunction
         Robert Mitchel &) - Defts.)
         Thomas Ingram   )   )

On a petition filed by Joel Shropshire one of the complainants in the above cause a Fiat for an injunction here to fore was made thereon and a writ of Injunction Subpoena and copy of said Petition issued agreeably to the prayer thereof, which fiat the defendants counsel moved to set and on argument thereon, the Court took an advisari untill Tomorrow.

Ordered by the Court that Joseph Boid be committed to the <u>Joal</u> of District of Washington for contempt, untill Tomorrow nine o'clock.

       Court adjourned untill Tomorrow nine o'clock.

David Campbell
Andrew Jackson
H. L. White

(p-312)   Saturday March the 19th 1803, Court met according to adjournment.
Present the Honorable

David Campbell)
Andrew Jackson) Esquires
Hugh L. White)

Ephraim Wilson - Compt.)
      vs   ) Bill & Injunction
Samuel Vance   - Deft.)

This cause dismissed by the complainant.

Robertsons Executors ≡ Compts.)
      vs   ) Retained as an original
Thomas Gillispie   - Defts.)

This day the above cause came on to be heard and on examination of the Bill
and Answer and Testimony on behalf of the complainant, It is ordered by the
Court that the Injunction in the above cause be perpetuated as to the twenty
Dollars and that the said Thomas Gillispie pay back to the complainants the
ballance of the Judgment obtained by him at Law and that he pay all costs
which hath occurred in this Court and that a decree be prepared accordingly.

(p-313)   Hudson Johnston & ╏ - Compts.)
         Joel Shropshire))
              vs   ) Bill & Injunction
         Richard Mitchel & ╏ - Defts.))
         Thomas Ingram))

On the motion made yesterday by the Defendants Council to Set aside the Fiat,
in this cause, and continued on an advisari untill today on argument. It is
the opinion of the Court that they take nothing by the motion and that the
cause now be taken up for final hearing, whereupon the complainants Bill and
Defendants Answer being read and on argument of Council on both sides the
Court took time to advise thereon untill next term.

William Cocke - Compt.)
      vs   ) Bill & Injunction
Armstead Blevins & James Kain - Defts.)

This day the above cause came on to be heard the complainants Bill and the
Answer of James Kain one of the Defendants being read. It is ordered by the
Court that the Injunction of the complainant be Dissolved and on motion
ordered that the Bill be retained as an original.

Lawrence Horn - Compt.)
    · vs   ) Bill & Injunction
Thomas Gibbons - Deft.)

This day the above cause came on ⌄o be heard, and on reading Bill and Answer
it is ordered by the Court that the Injunction of the Complainant be perpetuated for the sum of one hundred & two Dollars & eighty five cents, and

<u>Dessolved</u> as to the remainder and that each party pay his own cost in this
Court & that a decree be prepared to that effect.

(p-314)   Thomas Jackson - Compt.)
                    vs   ) Bill & Injunction
          John Honeycutt - Defts.)

It appearing to the Satisfaction of the Court that a publication hath heretofore been made agreeable to a rule of Last Term for the Defendant to appear
and file his answer at this Term. It is therefore ordered by the Court that
the Bill of the complainant be taken pro confesso accordingly.

Thomas King - Compt.)
          vs   ) Bill & Injunction
John McCaughan - Deft.)

It appearing to the Satisfaction of the Court that a publication in this cause
hath been inserted agreeable to a rule made at last Term, and the Defendant
thereupon failing to file his answer agreeably. It is ordered by the Court
that the Bill of the complainant be taken pro confesso.

John Bell - Compt.)
          vs   ) Original Bill
William Dewoody - Deft.)

This day the above cause came on to be heard, the complainants Bill being read,
and the Defendant having Demured thereto which was also read, whereupon the
Court were of opinion that the Demurrer be over Ruled.

(p-315)   Jacob & Henry Gyer - Compts.)
                    vs   ) Bill & Injunction
          John Teadlock   - Deft.)

This day the above cause came on to be heard and on reading the complainants
Bill and Defendants Answer. It is ordered by the Court that the Injunction
of the complainants be dissolved.

Lawrence Horn - compt.)
          vs   .) Bill & Injunction
Thomas Gibbons - Deft.)

James Forgy being heretofore Summoned as a witness in the above cause on be-
half of the complainant and failing to appear as he was bound to do at Last
Term whereupon a forfeiture Ni si was entered against him for cause shewn.
It is ordered by the Court that the forfeiture ni si be set aside.

William Dewoody - Compt.)
          vs   ) Original Bill
Samuel Cowens Heirs - Defts.)

On motion of complainant by his Council ordered by the Court that Francis A.
Ramsey be guardian for William M. Cowan & Polly Pernal Cowan heirs of said
Samuel Cowan Deceased to <u>defind</u> said cause and that a copy of this order be
served on said Francis.

(p-316)   James Penny   - Compt.   )
                    vs   ) Bill & Injunction
          William P. Chester & others Defts.)

Time given by consent untill next Term for Defendants to answer, and the
Court then adjourned untill Court in Course.

David Campbell
Andrew Jackson

(p-317)   SEPTEMBER TERM 1803

At a Court of Equity begun and held in the State of Tennessee for the district
of Washington in the town of Jonesborough on the 14th day of September in the
year of our Lord 1803 and on the 28th year of American Independence.

Present the Honorable

David Campbell) Judges of
Hugh L. White) said Court

Michael Harrison - Compt.)
         vs   ) Retained as an original
William Murphy and) Defts.)
Isaac Thomas   )   )

This cause continued by consent of parties.

William Skillern - Compt.)
         vs   ) Bill & Injunction
Nicholas Hawkins - Deft.)

This cause continued untill tomorrow by consent of parties.

(p-318)   Moses Humphreys - Compt.)
              vs   ) Bill and Injunction
          Armstead Blevins - Deft.)

On the 14th day of September 1803 the foregoing cause came on to be heard when
also came a jury, to wit, Thomas Ingram, Saml Wilson, John Thompson, William
Paine, Larken Webb, John Newman, John Poland, Joseph Owen, William Keer,
Robert Love, Joseph Rhea, William Brice who being empannelled and sworn to
try the issues of fact in this cause, to wit, 1st Did said Armstead send a
note to the jury informing them that he would release three hundred dollars,
or any other or what sum to induce them to find a verdict in his favour as
stated in complainants Bill? Did said Armstead after said verdict was rendered in his favour and before the end of that term agree with said complainant
to take one hundred or one hundred and fifty dollars in ful satisfaction of
said sum for which he had obtained a verdict and if so at what time and what
manner to be paid. We the jurors 1st do say we find that Armstead Blevins
did send a note to the jury agreeing to take two hundred and fifty dollars.
and release (p-319)   the ballance of the judgment if they would find a
verdict for him 2nd We find that on the same day after the return of the
verdict said Armstead Blevins did agree to take two hundred dollars in discharge of said judgment if it was paid without any further trouble, by paying
a horse worth one hundred dollars then an other hor e worth one hundred dollars
more in six months from that time.

The Court adjourned untill Tomorrow nine o'clock.

David Campbell
H. L. White

(p-320) Thursday the 15th of September A. Dom 1803
     Court met according to adjournment
          Present the Honorable
               David Campbell) Judges
               Hugh L. White   )

William Skellern - Compt.)
     vs   ) Bill & Injunction
Nicholas Hawkins - Deft.)

On the 15th day of September 1803 the foregoing cause came on to be heard
when also came a jury to wit.

Andrew Greer, Thomas Ingram, Samuel Wilson, John Thompson, William Paine,
Larken Webb, John Newman, John Poland, Joseph Owen, William Keer, Joseph
McCullock, Joseph Rhea who being empannelled and sworn to try the following
issues of fact in this cause to wit. Did the complainant collect all or
any part of the money arising from the sale of the said property in said
Bill mentioned, and what part and how and when did he dispose of such money.
We the jurors aforesaid do say we find that the complainant did receive a
part of the said money to wit forty dollars of George Brooks and four
(p-321) dollars of Patrick Cragan also that he did dispose of twenty one
dollars to the orders of Stockley Donalson Nathan Webb, John Webb and Moses
Webb.

William Christmas - Compt.)
     vs   ) Original Bill
Nathl & Samuel Henderson - Deft.)

This cause continued by consent of parties and that the defendant agree that
if the complainant is not ready for trial at the next term that the suit may
be continued untill September term 1804

Waightstill Avery - Compt.)
     vs   ) Original Bill
James Holland   - Deft.)

On the 15th day of September 1803 the foregoing cause on to be heard and on
affadavit being made by the complainant that Nathaniel Folsom and William
Cocke Samuel Wilson, John Colter are material witnesses for and on behalf of
the complainant its ordered by the Court that a commission De Be ne esse to
issue to take the testimony of the aforesaid witnesses and that one day
notice be given to the defendants atta. for Cocke and Folsom and that twenty
days notice be given to the defendants attorney to take the depositions of
Colter & Wilson.

(p-322) Rosanna Hamblin Executrix   )   )
         of the last Will and Testament) Compts.)
         of Daniel Hamblin deceased   )   )
                    vs   )   ) Bill & Injunction
              James Berry   -   Deft.)

On the 15th day of September 1803 the foregoing cause came on to be heard when also came a jury to wit. Robert Love, Henry Harkleroad, James Penny, Christopher Taylor, Francis Allison, John Parker, John Tipton Senr., John McGinnes, Dufty Jacobs, Charles Roberson, Benjamin Brown & Robert Allison, who being empannelled and sworn to try the issues of fact submitted in this cause by the order of the Court, to wit, of what value was the rent of the plantation mentioned in the complainants Bill, that James Berry agreed to convey to said complainant as stated in said Bill for the year beginning February one thousand and seven hundred and ninety four and for each succeeding year untill March in the year one thousand eight hundred and one. We the jurors aforesaid. Do say we find the rent of said Land to be worth one hundred dollars for the year one thousand   (p-323)   Seven hundred and ninety four and for each year -succeeding untill the end of the year one thousand eight hundred: making seven years.

Court adjourned untill tomorrow 9 o'clock.

                        David Campbell
                        H. L. White

Friday September 16th A. Dom 1803
     The Court met according to adjournment.
                        Present the Honorable
                             David Campbell) Judges
                             Hugh L. White)

Lawrence Horn - Compt.)
      vs   ) Bill in Equity
Thomas Gibbons - Deft.)

This cause coming on to be heard on the nineteenth day of March and now on this 16th day of September 1803 on the Bill and answer and exhibits and the evidence produced by the complainant and Defendant which, and the arguments of Council on both sides being heard examined and considered by the Court. It is thereupon ordered adjudged   (p-324)   and decreed by the Court that the Injunction heretofore granted in this cause to Stay and injunction the said Thomas Gibbons the Defendant his agents attornies and all persons concerned from all further proceedings on said Judgment recovered by the said Thomas against said complainant in said Court of pleas and Quarter Sessions for the County of Hawkins at August Term 1796 for the sum of one hundred and forty Eight Dollars and costs which is Stated in the complainants Bill, be perpetuated as to the sum of one hundred and two Dollars and eighty five cents part of said Judgment and that the said Injunction be Dissolved as to the remainder of said Judgment and it is further ordered adjudged and Decreed that the complainant pay his own costs in this Court and that the Defendant pay his own costs in this Court.
Test   David Campbell
John Carter C. & M. E.   Andrew Jackson
                               H. L. White

(p-325)   Richard Woods   )
              vs   )   In Equity
          Batt Wood, Thomas Wood)
          and Benjamin Gist   )

This cause having come on to be heard on the Seventeenth day of March last & continued on advisari untill this Eighteenth day of the same month & now on

this Sixteenth day of September 1803 on the bill & answers and the exhibits
& the evidence produced by the parties complainant & defendants and the Issues
that were tried & found by a Jury in this cause and the argument of Council
on both sides being heard examined & considered by the Court; it is thereupon
ordered adjudged & Decreed by the Court that the grant to Batt Wood mentioned
in the complainants bill so far as it covers land included within complainants
claim as described in his bill be and is declared void & of no effect & also
that the grant to Benjamin Gist Stated in complainants bill so far as it
covers land included in the said complainants claim by entry described in his
bill as aforesaid be and   (p-326)   is declared void null & of no effect,
and it is further ordered adjudged & deemed that an order be certified from
this court by the Clerk thereof to the Secretary of the State of North Carolina
or proper officer impowered to issue such warrant authorising and directing
a warrent to Issue to complainant. Richard Woods for said land described in
complainants Bill according to his Entry that a grant may Issue thereon to
him for the same and it is further decreed that the said defendants Batt Wood s
Thomas Woods and Benjamin Gist pay all costs that have accured on this cause
both at Law & in this Court. In witness whereof we the Judges of the said
Court have hereto subscribed our names in open Court this 16th Sept. 1803.

                              David Campbell
Test   Andrew Jackson
John Carter C.& M.E.   E. L. White

(p-327)   Hudson Johnston &) Compts.)
          Joel Shropshire   )   )
                  vs   )   ) Bill and Injunction
          Richard Mitchel &) Defts.)
          Thomas Ingram   )   )

This cause being continued at last Term on advisari came on this day for final
hearing and on argument it is ordered by the Court that the Bill be dismissed
with costs.

William Skellern - Compt.)
        vs   ) Bill and Injunction
Nicholas Hawkins - Deft.)

This day the above cause came on for final hearing and on argument it is
ordered by the court that the Bill be Dismissed with costs.

William Russell & others.- Compt.)
            vs   ) Bill & Injunction
Joseph Blair & others   - Defts.)

This day the above came on to be heard and on argument it is ordered to be
continued untill next term by consent of parties.

(p-328)   Thomas Jackson - Compt.)
                vs   ) Bill & Injunction
          John Hunnicut   - Deft.)

This day the above cause came on to be heard on a Rule Taken at last Term for
Taking the Bill pro confesso and on argument of Council it is ordered by the
Court that the suit be set for hearing at next Term and continued accordingly.

Thomas King - Compt.)
      vs   )   Bill & Injunction
John McCaughan - Deft.)

This day the above cause came on to be heard on a Rule Taken at last Term for
Taking the Bill pro confesso and on argument of Council it is ordered by the
Court that the suit be set for hearing at next Term and continued accordingly.

Allen Gillespie - Compt.   )
      vs   )   Original Bill
Samuel Piercifield & others - Defts.)

This day the above cause came on to be heard and on argument of the exceptions
to Samuel   (p-329)   Percifields answer it is ordered by the Court that the
exceptions be over Ruled.

James Crawford - Compt.   )
      vs   )   Original Bill
Charles Robertson Executors) Deft.)
and John Tadlock   )   )

The amended Bill filed. Time for James Gordan and Charles Robertson two of
the defendants to plead answer or Demur.

William Cobb - Compt.   )
      vs   )   Original Bill
William Conway & others - Deft.)

Death of the complainant suggested. On motion of complainants Council to receive the suit in the names of Sally Cobb and William Pharoah Cobb Heirs and
representatives of the said William Cobb decd. by three Guardians to wit
Pharoah Cobb Guardian of Sally Cobb and Sally Cobb Guardian of William P. Cobb
ordered by the Court that this cause stand revived in the names of Sally Cobb
and William P. Cobb Heirs and representatives of the said William Cobb Deceased by this Guardian aforesaid.

(p-330)   Charles Robertson and James   )   ) Bill
          Gordon Executors of the last Will   ) Compts.) in
          and Testament of Chal Robertson decd.)   ) Equity
                        vs   )   ) Decree
          Thomas Gillespie   - Deft.   )   )

The above cause having come on the nineteenth day of March 1803 and now again
coming on to be heard on the 16th day of September 1803 on the Bill, Answer,
and Testimony produced by the complainant, which and the arguments of Council
for the parties being heard examined and considered by the Court It is thereupon ordered adjudged and decreed by the Court that the Injunction heretofore
Granted in this cause to stay and enjoin the said Thomas the Defendant his
agents attorney and all persons concerned from all further proceedings on
said Judgment recovered by said Defendant against Charles Robertson deceased
the Testator of the complainants, in said Superior Court for the District of
Washington and revived at March   (p-331)   Term 1891 of said Court by the
Defendant against the complainants for the sum of one hundred and Sixty four
Dollars and Sixteen cents and costs which is Stated in the Bill of the Complainant be perpetuated as to Twenty Dollars part of said Judgment Stated in
the Bill of the complainants to have been paid by Charles Robertsons decd in

his lifetime to John Rhea Esqr. and that the said Defendant Thomas enter Satisfaction on the record of the Superior Court of Law for the District of Washington for one hundred and forty four Dollars and Sixteen cents the ballance of said Judgment recovered by said Defendant against Said Charles Robertson in his lifetime and revived against the complainants at March Term 1801 of said Court.

It is further ordered adjudged and Decreed that the Defendant pay to the complainants the Sum of Thirty nine Dollars and Fifty cents which   (p-332)   which they have heretofore paid for costs in the above cause and that the said Defendt pay all other costs that has accrued in said cause. In testimony of which we the Judges of said Court have here unto set our hand in open Court the 16th day of September 1803.

David Campbell
H. L. White

Test
John Carter C.M.E.
Court adjourned untill Court in course.

David Campbell
Andrew Jackson
H. L. White

(p-333)   MARCH TERM 1804

Saturday March 10th 1804 Court met according to adjournment.
      Present the Honorable

David Campbell
Andrew Jackson
Hugh L. White

William Russell & others - Compts.)
     vs   )   Bill
Joseph Blair & others   - Defts.)

This day the above cause came on for final hearing and on reading the complainant Bill and defendants answer and hearing the Evidence and argument thereon. It is ordered by the Court that the complainants Bill, be dismissed with costs without prejudice.

Jacob and Henry Gyer - Compt.)
     vs   )   Bill and Injunction
John Teadlock   - Deft.)

This day the above cause came on to be heard and on reading the complainants Bill and the defendant Answer and on motion of Defendants Council its ordered by the Court that the injunction of the complainants be disolved on the defendants giving Security to the complainants to refund the money recovered at Law if the complainants should loose the land mentioned in their Bill and now retained as an original.

(p-334)   John Bell - Compt.   )
               vs   )   Original Bill
          William Dewoudy - Deft.)

Continued & by consent of parties publication enlarged untill August Rule day next.

James Penny - Compt.   )
        vs   ) Bill and Injunction
William P. Chester, George Miller, Henry Miller)
& Jacob Miller Junior   )

Ordered by the Court that publication be twice made in the Washington Adver-
tiserprinted in Jonesbo; that George Miller Henry Miller and Jacob Miller
Junior do appear and answer the complainant Bill by the first day of next
term otherwise the complainants Bill will be taken for confessed.

(p-335)   William Hall - Compt.   )
             vs   ) Sci facias
      Charles Robertson and Joseph Martin Bill) Defts.)
      for Michael Harrison   )   )

Ordered by the Court that Judgment be entered according to Sci facias.
Court then adjourned untill Monday nine oclock.   David Campbell
                                         Andrew Jackson
                                         H. L. White
Monday the 12th March 1804 Court met according to adjournment.
     Present the Honorable
             David Campbell
             Andrew Jackson
             H. L. White

(p-336)   Robert Allison - Compt.   ) In Equity
             vs   ) order &
      Isaac Shelby William Hughes and Elizabeth Hughes) Decree

This cause having come on the 17th & 18th days of March one thousand eight
hundred and three before the Honorable David Campbell Andrew Jackson and Hugh
L. White Judges and now on this day before the said David Campbell Andrew
Jackson and Hugh L. White to be heard on the Bill of the complainant the
answers of the Defendants and exhibits filed in said Cause and it appearing
to the Court that a Jury being impanneled to try whether the purchase of the
said tract of land of two hundred acres mentioned in the said Bill of complainant by the said Elizabeth Hughs of the said Isaac Shelby as sheriff was
fraudulent or not found at September Term 1802 of this Honorable Court that
the purchase by said Elizabeth Hughs now Elizabeth Woods was not fraudulent
whereupon and upondebate of the matter in the presence of the Council for
both parties It is ordered adjudged and decreed by the Court that the Bill of
the complainant so far as it respects the said Elizabeth and the said Isaac
Shelby be dismissed. That the said complainant pay all costs so far as respects the said Elizabeth. That the said complainant and said Isaac Shelby
each pay their own costs so far as said Bill respects said Isaac; and it
is further ordered adjudged and decreed.   (p-337)   Andrew Jackson
                                              H. L. White

                            E N D

Note: Page numbers in this index refer to those of the original volume from which this copy was made. These numbers are inserted within parentheses throughout the text, as (p 124)

Berry, James, 84, 91, 98, 106,
    114, 121, 128, 129, 139,
    151, 164, 178, 191, 198,
    212, 267, 280, 304, 322
Berry, Thomas, 16, 32, 71, 84,
    194
Berry, Thos., 96
Berry, William, 84
Bishop, Joseph, 104
Blackburn, Archibald, 47, 174,
    189, 206, 218, 222, 235,
    248, 249, 257
Blair, Brice, 271, 277, 279
Blair, Bruce, 210
Blair, John, 16, 56, 250
Blair, Joseph, 160, 173, 188,
    189, 205, 220, 233, 259,
    288, 302, 327, 333
Blair, William, 218
Blevins, Armsted, 240
Blevins, Armstid, 264, 290,
    301, 318, 319, 313
Blevins, Dellin, 74
Blevins, Dillen, 59
Blevins, John, 118, 124, 133,
    143, 154, 168, 183, 201,
    215, 230, 255, 282
Blevins, William, 5, 6, 13, 15,
    22, 23, 26, 34, 35, 37, 38,
    49, 70, 74, 78, 183, 184
Blount, William, 1, 11, 33, 55
Blount, Wm., 1
Blountville, 93
Boggess, Bennett, 209
Boid, Joseph, 311
Booth, David, 83, 90, 98, 105,
    114, 121, 128, 138
Boothe, David, 30, 43, 53, 62,
    68, 149
Bounds, Jesse, 47, 48
Bragg, David, 302
Brice, William, 318
Brindle, Richard, 12
Britain, Joseph, 59
Brittain, Joseph, 87
Britton, Joseph, 16, 56
Bromley, Augustine, 40, 48
Brooks, George, 320
Brooks, Jane, 209, 224, 237, 245
Brown, Benjamin, 322
Brown, Jacob, 150, 213, 214, 271,
    276, 277, 279
Brown, John, 5, 6, 13, 23, 35, 74,
    78, 245
Brown, Joseph, 242
Brown, Ruth, 10, 93, 101, 108, 116,

Brown, Ruth (cont), 123, 130, 141,
    152, 166, 180, 199, 213, 229,
    254
Brown, Thomas, 218
Brumley, Augustine, 14, 28, 60, 65
Bryant, James, 21, 30
Buchanan, John, 24
Bull, John, 10, 18, 22
Bullard, Isaac, 11
Bullard, Joseph, 21, 30
Bullock, Leonard H., 3, 15, 26
Bullock, Leonard Henley, 291, 292,
    293, 297, 298
Bullock, Richard, 177, 296, 297, 298
Burk, William, 134, 144, 155
Burke, William, 169, 185, 202, 216
Burlison, Aaron, 47, 48
Burum, Henry, 208

C

Cage, Jas., 194
Caldwel, Benoni, 134
Caldwell, Benoni, 144, 155, 169, 184
Caldwell, Bennoni, 202
Caldwell, David, 46, 47
Calvert, William, 302
Campbell, Arthur Colonel, 219
Campbell, David, 1, 2, 10, 11, 21, 33,
    34, 35, 38, 45, 55, 64, 65, 68,
    72, 78, 86, 126, 136, 148, 161,
    176, 196, 211, 228, 243, 245,
    247, 249, 251, 252, 257, 258,
    259, 264, 270, 271, 274, 275,
    276, 278, 279, 280, 283, 286,
    287, 289, 291, 299, 300, 301,
    304, 305, 306, 311, 312, 316,
    317, 319, 320, 323, 324, 326,
    332, 333, 334, 335, 336
Campbell, Robert, 106, 194, 209,
    224, 237, 262, 288
Campbell, William, 24
Carnes, Judge, 203
Carney, John, 28, 41, 64, 69, 82, 89,
    97, 105, 113, 121, 127, 137,
    149, 164, 178, 196
Carr, William, 271, 277, 279
Carrick, Moses, 125, 133, 143, 155,
    169, 184, 201, 216, 230, 244,
    255, 283, 309
Carson, John Colonel, 123
Carter, Caleb, 12, 22
Carter, John, 74, 110, 111, 200, 275,
    276, 292, 324, 326, 332
Carter, Landon, 16, 34, 55, 139, 146,
    275, 292, 295

Engle, George, 180, 181
English, Andrew, 4, 8, 15, 17,
    27, 37, 48, 59, 65, 95,
    197, 213
English, James, 195, 218
Erwin, Benjamin, 118
Erwin, Edward, 118
Erwine, Benjamin, 110, 124, 132, 142,
    154, 167, 181, 182
Erwine, Edward, 110, 124, 132, 142,
    154, 167, 181, 182
Evans, Jesse, 94, 141
Evans, John B., 159, 172
Evans, William, 87, 90, 109, 117,
    123, 131

F

Fagan, John, 23, 93
Feagan, John, 84
Fegan, John, 40, 50, 61, 93,
    100, 101, 108, 116, 183
Feugan, John, 66
Fitzgarald, Garret, 149
Fitzgarrald, Garret, 62
Fitzgarrald, Garrett, 83, 105
Fitzgerald, Garet, 114
Fitzgerald, Garret, 90, 98, 121,
    128, 138
Fitzgerald, Garrett, 43, 53
Fitzgerrald, Garrit, 195
Fitzgerrald, Gerrett, 30, 68
Flat Creek, 14
Fletcher, John Gold, 208
Folsom, Nathaniel, 321
Ford, Benjamin, 30, 43, 53, 62,
    68, 83, 90, 98, 105, 114,
    121, 128, 138, 149, 195
Forgey, James, 286, 302
Fowler, John, 22, 24

G

Gaines, Frances H., 269
Gaines, James, 87, 90, 135
Galbreaith, James, 209, 271, 282
Galbreath, James, 150, 166
Galbreath, Jas., 14
Gardener, William, 63, 113, 137
Gardiner, William, 54
Gardner, William, 69, 77, 81, 88,
    97, 105, 120, 127, 149, 162,
    163, 177, 196
Garner, Brice M., 271, 277, 279
Garrett, Joseph, 302, 303
Gass, John, 182, 183, 192, 207,

Gass, John (cont), 213, 223, 236,
    262, 288, 310
George Town, 159
Georgia, 5, 171, 186, 203, 217, 225,
    232, 295
Gest, Benjamin, 92, 100, 107, 116,
    122, 130, 140
Gibbons, Thomas, 159, 173, 188, 194,
    205, 209, 220, 224, 233, 237,
    261, 262, 286, 288, 313, 315,
    323, 324
Gilaspie, Thomas, 47
Gillaland, John, 63, 68
Gillaspie, Geo., 71
Gillenwater, Joel, 56, 59, 134, 155,
    169, 184, 202
Gillespie, Allen, 227, 240, 261
Gillespie, Thomas, 241, 265, 300, 312
Gilliland, John, 42, 53, 71, 83, 90,
    94
Gillingwater, Joel, 144
Gillispie, Allen, 290, 328
Gillispie, Thomas, 330, 331
Gist, Benjamin, 152, 165, 179, 199,
    208, 213, 229, 243, 247, 271,
    272, 273, 281, 306, 308, 325,
    326
Glascock, Archibald, 302
Goodman, Alexander, 22
Goodson, John, 269
Goodwin, Benjamin, 10, 18, 22
Gordon, James, 197, 210, 241, 246,
    265, 329, 330
Gray, Robt., 195
Gregg, James, 277
Greenlee, James, 93, 102
Greer, Alexander, 106
Greer, Alexd., 65
Greer, Andrew, 59, 85, 91, 92, 99,
    106, 107, 115, 135, 139, 150,
    151, 165, 179, 182, 197, 198
    212, 277, 279, 302, 320
Greer, Andrew Senior, 85, 91, 98,
    106, 107, 115, 122, 129
Greer, Jos., 27
Greer, Joseph, 8, 9, 14
Greer, William, 217, 232
Grissum, Archibald, 217, 232
Gwin, Robert, 84
Gyer, Henry, 268, 315, 333
Gyer, Jacob, 210, 268, 315, 333

H

Hacket, John, 70, 82
Hackett, John, 8, 89

E N D

www.ingramcontent.com/pod-product-compliance
Lightning Source LLC
Chambersburg PA
CBHW021830020426
42334CB00014B/557